Parliament

Canada's Democracy and How It Works

Also by Maureen McTeer

Residences: Homes of Canada's Leaders

Parliament

Canada's Democracy
and
How It Works

by Maureen McTeer

Random House of Canada

Revised Edition, 1995

Originally published in 1987 by Random House of Canada Limited.

Canadian Cataloguing in Publication Data

McTeer, Maureen, 1952-
Parliament: Canada's democracy and how it works

Rev. ed.
ISBN: 0-394-22462-0

1. Canada. Parliament. 2. Canada – Politics and government.
3. Canada – Constitutional law.
I. Title.

JL136.M37 1995   320.971   C95-930009-0

Cover by Sharon Foster Design
Cover photograph courtesy of CANAPRESS
Interior design by Sharon Oda
Illustrations by Peter Grau

Printed and bound in Canada.
10 9 8 7 6 5 4 3 2 1

Acknowledgements

Since the publication of the original version of *Parliament: Canada's Democracy and How It Works* there have been many changes in the workings of government, in the procedures of the House of Commons and the Senate, and in Canada. I wish to thank all those people who took the time originally, and in the past few months, to help ensure this book is as complete and current as possible. Their assistance is most appreciated and, as always, I accept full responsibility for any mistakes.

To Joe, who has taught me so much about this subject;
and to Catherine, so that she too can learn
about how we are governed.

Table of Contents

Introduction

CANADA IS the largest democratic country in the world. To make that democracy work across all our regions and for all Canadians is a constant challenge.

At the heart of our democratic system is Parliament. It is here, in this truly national forum, that laws are passed. Here, all Canadians in every region can be heard, through elected Members of Parliament in the House of Commons and through appointed Senators in the Senate.

I believe that more Canadians — especially young Canadians — should understand how our system of government works. That is why I have written this book. Our democratic system is real and exciting and dynamic. I think that the more you learn about how we are governed, the more you will want to become actively involved in that process yourself.

We will begin with a brief tour of the Centre Block, where the House of Commons and the Senate are located. I hope that someday you will have the chance to take this tour in person. But for now, we will start in front of the Centre Block, near the eternal flame. Follow the diagram to see where we are along the way.

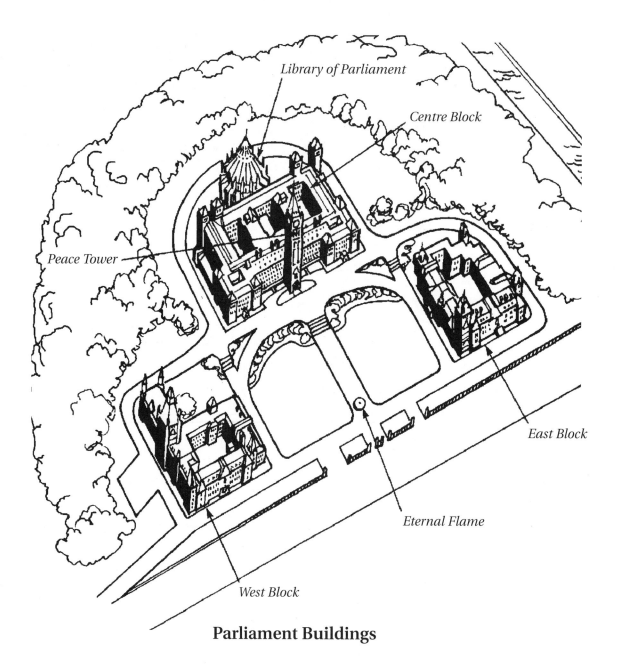

Library of Parliament

Centre Block

Peace Tower

East Block

Eternal Flame

West Block

Parliament Buildings

Welcome to the Parliament Buildings

ON JULY 1, 1867, Canada became a nation. On New Year's Eve, 100 years later, Prime Minister Lester B. Pearson stood with hundreds of other Canadians in front of the Parliament Buildings in Ottawa, Canada's capital city. As the bells of the Peace Tower rang in Canada's Centennial year, he lit the eternal flame, which still burns today. It is surrounded by the emblems of the ten provinces and two territories that make up Canada.

As we stand beside the eternal flame, we are directly in front of the Centre Block of the Parliament Buildings. The West Block is to our left and the East Block is to our right. Members of Parliament (MPs) and Senators have their offices in these three buildings and also in the Wellington, Victoria and Confederation buildings, nearby on Wellington Street.

Ahead of us, along a wide avenue, are steps that lead to the main doors of the Centre Block. On the left is a private entrance for MPs leading directly to the House of Commons. A similar private entrance on the right serves Senators and leads to the Senate Chamber.

When you are close enough to the building, stop and study the Peace Tower. It was built as a memorial to Canadians who were killed in World War I. The tower stands 90 m (300 feet) high to the base of the flagpole and contains 53 bells. The largest weighs 10,160 kg (22,400 pounds) and the smallest weighs 4.5 kg (10 pounds). These bells are arranged in a *carillon* so that music can be played on them. Every day at 12:45 p.m., the Dominion Carilloneur plays a 15-minute concert. On certain days — like Canada Day — longer concerts are played.

At the top of the Peace Tower is a huge four-faced clock whose chimes ring every 15 minutes. The chime of the huge clock is the same as Big Ben's in London, England.

Centre Block/Peace Tower
Parliament Buildings

Below the clock is a glassed-in observation deck to allow visitors a chance to see the city from 57 m (187 feet) above the ground. The open, windy observation deck was closed after two people jumped to their deaths from it in 1970. I can remember visiting the open observation deck as a child and being terrified that the cold and howling wind would blow me away, like Dorothy in *The Wizard of Oz*.

Something To Do

Need Some Help to Plan Your Trip to Ottawa?

Many schools visit the Nation's Capital each year. To help you plan your trip, the National Capital Commission will send you a free package describing things to do while you are there.

Write to: National Capital Commission
           161 Laurier Avenue West
           Ottawa, Ontario
           K1P 6J6
           Attention: Visitor's Centre

Your Member of Parliament can also help. For instance, your MP can:

☞ send you pamphlets on the House of Commons and the Senate;

☞ make special arrangements for your group to meet and ask questions of a senior parliamentarian, such as a Cabinet Minister from your province or region;

☞ make special arrangements for your group to eat in one of the restaurants run by the House of Commons;

☞ arrange for your group to have a specially guided tour of the Centre Block and of the Heritage rooms in the East Block;

☞ book up to 50 seats for your group in the public gallery of the House of Commons; and

☞ provide you with small lapel pins of the Canadian flag to help identify your group.

THE MAIN ENTRANCE AND CONFEDERATION HALL

A stately arch looms over the main entrance to the Centre Block. If you were on a regular tour of Parliament, you would meet your guide here, just inside the main door, on the steps leading up to the Confederation Hall.

I first came to visit Parliament when I was a nine-year-old Brownie. Since then, I have walked through the Confederation Hall hundreds of times. Yet, even today, I am still awed by the intricate stonework depicting our Canadian heritage. If you can, take the time to look around this high-ceilinged circular chamber. Almost every detail has a special meaning. For instance, the huge central column, with the ten arches above it, is said to represent Canada's ten provinces. Carvings represent Canada's Aboriginal peoples as well as early arrivals from Europe, including sailors, trappers, and *coureurs-de-bois* (woodsmen). There are also carvings of Canadian flowers and wildlife.

On the floor, around the base of the central column, is a mariner's (sailor's) compass. The dark marble between the 16 points of the compass symbolizes the sun. Around this is a circle of grey marble that represents the world. Finally, a wavy outer band symbolizes the seas — the lifelines of Canada as a trading nation.

THE SPEAKER'S PARADE

Between September and June, when Parliament is in session, you can watch the daily Speaker's Parade. It passes through the Confederation Hall on its way to the House of Commons. First come constables from the security staff. They are followed by the Sergeant-at-Arms, the Commons' chief security officer. This officer carries the Mace — the symbol of Parliament's authority. Behind the Sergeant-at-Arms walks the Speaker, dressed in a black gown, white gloves and a three-cornered black hat. Beside the Speaker is a page bearing the prayer for the day, and following behind are the Clerk of the House of Commons and several Clerks Assistant.

They are on their way to open the daily session of the House of Commons. Part of that session is the daily Question Period when the Prime Minister and Cabinet Ministers are questioned by both opposition and government Members of Parliament. It is all part of our tradition of responsible government, in which the Prime Minister and Cabinet Ministers must account for their actions and decisions, through Parliament, to the people of Canada. (We'll be learning more about Question Period later in the book.)

THE
LIBRARY OF
PARLIAMENT

Anyone who enters the library looks immediately toward the ceiling at the cupola — a glass dome 40 m (132 feet) above the floor. Underneath the cupola is a white marble statue of Queen Victoria, one of England's best-loved monarchs, who reigned from 1837 to 1901. She was also the queen who chose Ottawa to be Canada's capital city.

If you have a sweet tooth, try to avoid the miniature replica (copy) of the library that stands on a table near the entrance. A chef of the parliamentary restaurant made it entirely of sugar to celebrate the library's 100th anniversary in 1976.

The Library of Parliament was completed in 1876. It now houses more than 650,000 books and manuscripts. It is mainly reserved for use by MPs, Senators and their staffs. Other people, such as journalists, teachers and students, can also use the library if given permission by the head librarian. Some of the books can be borrowed.

In 1952, an electrical fire caused so much water damage to the library that it had to be almost completely redone. Hundreds of books had to be dried on special clotheslines, using huge dehumidifiers that absorbed over 1000 L (about 240 gallons) of water every day for three months!

Library of Parliament

The Great Fire of 1916

On the evening of February 3, 1916, a raging fire destroyed the original Centre Block of the Parliament Buildings, killing seven people. No one ever discovered how the fire was started among the hundreds of newspapers and magazines in the Reading Room used by MPs and Senators. The Library of Parliament was the only part of the building saved. A quick-thinking employee rushed to close the huge iron doors at its entrance, moments before the fire could spread to the thousands of precious books inside.

The present Centre Block of the Parliament Buildings was opened on February 26, 1920, by the Duke of Devonshire, who was then Canada's Governor General.

Under Construction

The Centre Block of the Parliament Buildings is still being completed. When it was built, many pieces of limestone were left blank. Parliamentary sculptress Eleanor Milne has worked since 1962 to have some of these blank stones carved — including a 16-panel frieze in the foyer of the House of Commons depicting Canada's history. In 1980, nine Aboriginal sculptors made carvings over a number of entranceways in the Centre Block.

THE
MEMORIAL
CHAMBER

One level up from the Library of Parliament, in the Peace Tower, is the Memorial Chamber. At its entrance are two stone lions, each supporting a shield. One shield bears the dragon of war and the other the dove of peace. This chamber was built of materials from Great Britain, France and Belgium, the three main countries where Canadians served during World War I (1914–1918). It was officially opened to the public on November 11, 1928, by Prime Minister Mackenzie King.

In the middle of the room is an altar chiselled from a single piece of English Yorkshire limestone. On it is the Book of Remembrance, which contains the names and military ranks of the 66,655 Canadian men and women who died on foreign soil during World War I. Four other books have since been added to honour Canadians who were killed in other wars in which Canada was formally involved. These include the Nile Expedition (1884–1885), the South African War (1899–1902), World War II (1939–1945) and the Korean War (1950–1953).

Each day at 11 a.m. there is a brief ceremony in the Memorial Chamber. This is the hour of the Armistice (or truce) that ended World War I on the "eleventh hour of the eleventh day of the eleventh month," in 1918. During the ceremony, House of Commons security personnel quietly turn the pages of the five books in the Chamber. In this way, the name of each soldier listed in them can be visible to the public at least once a year. If a member of your family was killed during these wars, the security personnel will tell you on what day his or her page will be visible. You can also order a duplicate copy of the page to be sent to you.

At a time when so many of us are concerned about the horrors of war, this special room — set aside in the very heart of the Peace Tower — is an important symbol. It is a memorial to those Canadians who fought in past wars to defend our democratic rights and freedoms. It is also a reminder to each of us today that we must guard our freedoms and work for peace.

Need some information for your school projects? The Public Information Office of the House of Commons has many fact sheets, brochures, booklets, videos and kits which can be of help to you. You can write to them for a full list of what is available at:

Public Information Office
House of Commons
Ottawa, Canada, K1A 0A6
(613) 992-4793 or fax (613) 992-1273

Furred and Feathered Heroes

Over the entrance to the Memorial Chamber are the carved heads of a pack mule, a horse, a reindeer, a dog, carrier pigeons, mice and canaries — the animals who helped the soldiers during World War I. The memorial to the animals reads: "The humble beasts, who also served and died." Many people — including me — have asked why the field mice and canaries are there. The answer I received is that during World War I, the "tunnelers' friends," as the mice and canaries were called, were carried around by the soldiers when they were in the trenches (deep cuts in the earth where they were sheltered from enemy bombardment). During a gas attack, the mice and canaries suffocated and died quickly, warning of gas in the air. The soldiers could then try to escape the deadly gas by putting on their gas masks.

THE
HOUSE OF
COMMONS

The House of Commons is the political nerve centre of Canada. In this truly national forum, Members of Parliament fulfill an important part of their responsibilities as your elected representatives. Since 1977, the daily sittings of the House of Commons have been televised when Parliament is in session — usually between September and June. There is simultaneous translation of all MPs' speeches from English to French and vice versa.

As you can see from the diagram, the Speaker sits at the top of the chamber. The government Members sit on the Speaker's right and those from the opposition sit on the left. Cabinet and senior government Members sit in the front row, at desks made of hand-

House of Commons

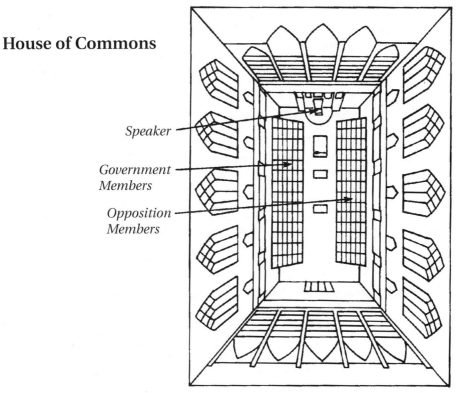

Speaker

Government Members

Opposition Members

carved Canadian oak. Facing them are senior Members of the official Opposition party, who are often called the "shadow cabinet." It is their responsibility to ask questions of Cabinet Ministers, and they could become Cabinet Ministers themselves if their party won a general election.

The Prime Minister and the Leader of the Opposition sit in the middle of the chamber, directly across from each other. Members of other parties sit on the left of (and farthest from) the Speaker. When there are too many government backbenchers for the government benches (as happened after the 1984 election), they sit with the opposition Members, across the floor from their own government colleagues.

13

The 11 galleries above the floor of the Commons can accommodate about 560 people. If you wanted to visit the House of Commons, you would sit here. Only MPs and persons with business in the House of Commons — such as Clerks, the Sergeant-at-Arms, the Hansard reporters and the pages — are allowed on the floor of the House of Commons. The rest of us are "strangers" and can be removed from the chamber at any time by the Sergeant-at-Arms. On two sides of the Commons Chamber are lobbies (rooms) that have telephones, desks and sofas — one for the use of government Members and one for the use of opposition parties.

In front of the Speaker's chair is the Clerks' table, where the Clerk and his or her Clerks' Assistant sit. The four small desks in the centre of the Commons Chamber are used for Hansard reporters. (Hansard is the formal record of the House of Commons.) The Sergeant-at-Arms sits at a small table nearest the door at the far end of the chamber from the Speaker.

A Victory for Canada's Diversity

Until 1973, every man sitting as an MP's guest in the Members' Gallery of the House of Commons had to wear a tie and jacket. That year, four Aboriginal people from Alberta wearing their traditional dress were asked to leave the Members' Gallery. As a result, their Member of Parliament, Joe Clark, spoke to Speaker Lucien Lamoureux, who agreed to change the dress rules. Canadian Aboriginal people can now wear their traditional clothes while watching Parliament's proceedings as guests of their MP.

In the red Senate Chamber, our 104 Senators meet when Parliament is in session. At one end of the room, under a canopy, are the Throne chairs. They are used by the Queen and Prince Philip when they are in Canada for the Opening of Parliament. Otherwise, they are used by the Governor General and his or her spouse. A bust of Queen Victoria is above the canopy.

The chair directly in front of the Throne chairs is used by the Speaker of the Senate. If the Queen is in the Senate chamber, the Speaker's regular chair is taken out, and a smaller one is placed in line with the Senators on the Queen's right. As in the House of Commons, the table at which the Clerks sit is directly in front of the Speaker's chair. Smaller desks are used by the reporters who record the Senators' speeches.

Senate Chamber

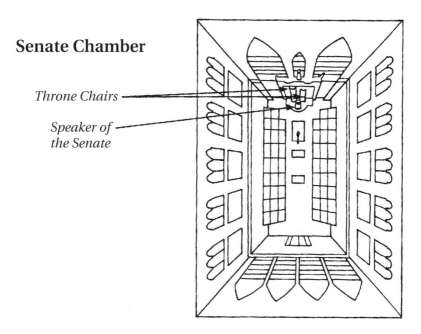

Throne Chairs

*Speaker of
the Senate*

The Gentleman Usher of the Black Rod, who is responsible for the Senate's security, sits at the far end of the chamber. Behind his desk is a brass railing, called the Bar of the Senate. MPs stand behind the railing to hear the Speech from the Throne and to watch Royal Assent being given to all bills before they become law. As in the Commons, government supporters are seated to the right of the Speaker and the opposition is to the left.

The Portrait with a Charmed Life

The huge painting of Queen Victoria in the Senate foyer has been saved from fire four times. In the 1840s, it hung above the Speaker's chair in the Parliament Buildings in Montreal. In 1849, following passage of the controversial Rebellion Losses Bill, a riot erupted and the building was set on fire. Four men went back into the fiery building to save the portrait of Queen Victoria.

The painting was temporarily housed in a local hotel. It had to be saved a second time when the hotel also burned down.

In February 1854, a fire broke out under the library in the Legislative council in Quebec City, where the painting of Queen Victoria had hung for three years. Although the building was destroyed, the painting was carried to safety a third time and put in the Centre Block in Ottawa in 1866. During the 1916 fire, a rescue party saved the painting for the fourth time. To make the story even more incredible, one of the Ottawa rescuers — Walter Todd — was the son of one of the men who had saved the Queen's portrait during the 1849 fire in Montreal!

Canada's System of Government

WHAT IS A
DEMOCRACY?

You have probably heard people say that Canada is a *democracy*. But what does this mean? Democracy is one way for a group of people to make decisions on what is best for the largest number of them — called the majority. The dictionary defines the word democracy as "rule or government by the people." This idea of people being in charge (or ruling) is the basic ingredient of a democratic system of government.

But how does democracy work in practice? In ancient Greece, in the city-state of Athens, every man had to take his turn at governing. In fact, each man was in charge of leading the government for part of each year. In that city, at that time, the people (the men, at least) really did "rule." Over the centuries, our system of democracy evolved and developed. Perhaps even today, if you live in a small village, you might take turns being the head of the town government for part of the year.

As life became more complex, though, and populations grew, democracy changed from a system of government by the people ruling *directly* to one where they ruled *indirectly* through *elected* representatives. These elected representatives were people from among their own community. This system of democracy or rule by elected representatives of the people is what we have in Canada today. Our representatives are freely elected by secret ballot (vote) by all Canadians in every part of Canada.

The tool we use to make our democracy work is the parliamentary system. At the federal level, this is made up of the elected House of Commons, the appointed Senate, and the Queen's representative, the Governor General. At the provincial level, we have the elected Legislatures. No provincial Legislature has an appointed upper house. The Lieutenant Governor in each province represents the Queen.

The rules both levels of government follow are basically the same. For instance, they have free elections about every four or five years. There are certain written rules each person must follow before and after being elected as an MP or a member of the provincial Legislature. Both levels of government have Cabinets — groups of senior elected government representatives. Cabinet Ministers are responsible (answerable) to the House of Commons or Legislature, and through these to the people who elected them. (This is called *responsible government*.)

If the people do not agree with the decisions made by their elected representatives, they can tell them so. The majority (50 percent of the voters plus one) can vote any elected representative out of his or her job at any election. The same electors can choose a new elected representative or re-elect the one they already have to speak out for their area. And the government *must*, by law, call elections. In our democracy, the elected representatives are indeed responsible to the people.

Canada's Symbols

Do you know how Canada got its name? Do you know the history and meaning of Canada's federal and provincial coats of arms and flags?

The Secretary of State's department has put together a colourful booklet about Canada's official symbols.

It costs about $4.95 and is available from the Canada Communication Group-Publishing, Ottawa, Canada, KlA 0S9, (819) 956-4802 or by fax at (819) 994-1498, or from any government bookstore.

Refer to Catalogue no. S2-211-1991-E.

Canada has a *federal* system of government. This means that there is more than one level of government with the power to make decisions and pass laws for the country. There is the federal (national) government, as well as ten provincial governments and two territorial governments (the Yukon and the Northwest Territories).

The Yukon and the Northwest Territories

The Yukon has a tradition of elections dating back to 1899, when thousands of adventurers and prospectors arrived to seek fortunes in the Klondike Gold Rush. The Territorial Council has been fully elected since 1908. But the federal government continued to administer the territory like a colony until 1979. A Commissioner, appointed by the federal government, served as chief executive officer. He (it was always a man) effectively ran the government on instructions from a federal minister. However, the elected people kept battling for control over their own affairs. Finally, in 1979, Ottawa put the elected members in charge of the Yukon's administration, and the Commissioner unofficially took on the duties of a Lieutenant Governor. The elected party leader became roughly equivalent to a provincial premier.

In the Northwest Territories, elections began in 1951. By 1983, the Territorial Council had grown to 24, all elected members. Unlike the Yukon, the appointed federal Commissioner is still the chief executive of the Northwest Territories. But an executive committee of eight elected members is the senior decision-making body. The powers of both territorial governments are now more equal to those of a provincial government, but full provincial status remains to be achieved.

Canada has a constitution — a basic set of rules by which we are governed. Canada's constitution is both written and unwritten. The written part is contained mainly in the *Constitution Act, 1982,* which brought our constitution home from England in a form that could be amended (changed) by the Canadian Parliament and the provincial Legislatures. The *British North America Act, 1867,* the original document that brought Canada into existence, and its various amendments are now called the *Constitution Acts, 1867–1982.* A *Charter of Rights and Freedoms* is also a vital part of Canada's written constitution.

The unwritten part of the constitution consists of parliamentary and other political customs and traditions. For instance, the positions of Prime Minister and Cabinet, political parties, and federal-provincial conferences are not mentioned in our written constitution. But we all know that these things are essential to the way we are governed.

Sections 91, 92 and 93–95 of the *Constitution Acts, 1867–1982* are the main sections dealing with divisions of power between the federal and provincial governments. This is usually called the *constitutional division of powers.* The federal government is responsible for all matters involving the whole country, such as foreign affairs, international trade and national economic policy. The provinces are responsible for things that affect each province individually, including education, the delivery of social services such as health care and hospitals, and highways within each province.

There are many areas where the federal and provincial governments share responsibilities, such as agriculture, justice, post-secondary education, the environment, family allowances and old age security.

Sometimes the federal and provincial governments disagree about whose jurisdiction (area of authority or legal power) is involved. For instance, what happens when a new activity, not mentioned in the constitution, comes along? Remember that when the Fathers of Confederation were drafting the original constitution before 1867, there were no airplanes, televisions, cars or radios. Because of this, no mention was made in the constitution about which level of government would be responsible for these new developments. As they occurred, our constitution had to change as well.

When there is a disagreement about jurisdiction that the two levels of government cannot resolve, they can ask the courts to decide. The federal government can go directly to the Supreme Court of Canada, and each province to its provincial court of appeal. The court then gives a constitutional decision, and the two sides must proceed according to the court's interpretation. Since it is impossible to know which way the court will decide, both sides will often prefer to negotiate an agreement on their own. That is one reason we have regular federal-provincial Ministers' Conferences. At these meetings, the Ministers can agree on solutions without going to court.

Something To Do

Are You a Philatelist?

Maybe you are without knowing it — a philatelist is a stamp collector!

Did you know that your Member of Parliament can help you with your collection? Here is how you can be put on the First Day of Issue list for all new stamps:

☞ Write your MP (or a Senator from your province) asking if he or she would write a letter on your behalf to the House of Commons post office.

☞ State whether you would like a single stamp or a "corner," which is a 4-stamp block. (Corners cost more.)

☞ Also state whether you want your stamps machine or hand cancelled or in "mint" condition — which means not cancelled at all.

☞ Your MP or Senator will then write to the Postmaster of the House of Commons, asking that your name be put on the list and explaining what you want.

☞ The philatelic clerk of the House of Commons will then write to you. It costs about $40 to set up an account for a "corner" and $20 for a single stamp. When your account gets low, the clerk will ask for another deposit to cover the cost of future stamps.

☞ On the first day that each new Canadian stamp is issued, you will get yours from the House of Commons post office.

☞ You can ask your MP for information about the Philatelic Museum in Ottawa. You might want to visit it if you come to the capital.

PARLIAMENTARY
GOVERNMENT
We now know that Canada is a democracy with a federal system of government, where decision-making and law-making powers are shared between the federal and provincial governments. But how are decisions made, and by whom? In Canada, we make democracy work through Parliament at the federal level, and through the Legislatures at the provincial level. This system of parliamentary democracy is the basis of how we are governed in Canada.

We will look now at how the federal Parliament works. With certain exceptions, similar rules apply to provincial Legislatures. There are three key elements (parts) of the parliamentary system in Canada. These are the Queen (represented by the Governor General), the elected House of Commons and the appointed Senate. Each has a role to play.

❦

The Hon. Eugene A. Forsey spent his life writing and lecturing on Canada's Constitution. A Senator from 1970 to 1979, he was named to the Privy Council in 1985. As a young law student, I can remember seeking his help for research in my course on constitutional law. Although Senator Forsey died in February 1991, students can still learn from him by reading his booklet *How Canadians Are Governed.*

For a copy, in either English or French, write to:
> Public Information Office
> House of Commons
> Ottawa, Canada,
> KlA 0A6

Refer to Catalogue no. X9-11/1991-E ISBN 0-662-17601-4

❦

The Governor General

THE OFFICE OF Governor General — Queen's representative in Canada — is the first element in the parliamentary system.

Today, the Governor General does not have real power except in very unusual emergencies. Over the years, power has been transferred from the Governor General to the Prime Minister and the Cabinet. The Prime Minister and Cabinet are also referred to as the Executive. This is because they execute (carry out) the plans and policies of government.

For many Canadians, though, the position of Governor General remains an important national symbol. The person who holds the position is respected and admired. The first Canadian-born Governor General was Vincent Massey, who held the position from 1952 to 1959. (Before that, our Governors General were from Great Britain.) The late Rt. Hon. Jeanne Sauvé was the first woman to serve as Governor General. She was appointed on May 14, 1984, for a five-year term. Her successor was the Rt. Hon. Ramon John Hnatyshyn. On February 8, 1995, the Rt. Hon. Roméo LeBlanc was sworn in as Canada's 25th Governor General. He is the first Acadian to serve as our Head of State.

Today the Governor General acts on the advice of the Prime Minister and the Cabinet, who are responsible through Parliament to the people of Canada. As part of his or her formal duties, the Governor General:

- gives Royal Assent to all Acts of Parliament;
- *signs orders-in-council and other state documents;*
- appoints as Prime Minister the party leader whose party elected the most MPs at a general election;
- appoints a new Prime Minister to hold office until a new leader can be chosen, if the Prime Minister dies or resigns;
- opens, prorogues and dissolves Parliament on the advice of the Prime Minister;
- reads the Speech from the Throne at the opening of Parliament;
- travels across Canada to attend all kinds of events, from winter carnivals to fancy dress balls;

Government House has many booklets, posters and fact sheets on Canada's Governors General, the Queen and Royal family and programs offered at Rideau Hall. For free copies, write to:

Information Services Directorate
Government House
1 Sussex Drive
Ottawa, Canada, KlA 0A1
(613) 993-9530 or fax (613) 990-7636

- ☞ receives people at the official residences — Rideau Hall in Ottawa and the Citadel in Quebec City — including foreign heads of state who are visiting Canada;
- ☞ travels to other countries, accompanied by a designated Cabinet Minister, to act as a goodwill ambassador and representative for Canada;
- ☞ meets regularly with the Prime Minister to discuss the government's plans;
- ☞ presents awards for bravery and outstanding achievement to Canadians.

Earl Grey

Sound like a kind of tea? Yes, indeed — but it was also the name of Canada's ninth Governor General (1904 – 1911). Among his many accomplishments, he encouraged the creation of the Department of External Affairs and suggested the restoration of Louisbourg in Nova Scotia as a historic site. Each fall, we watch our favourite football teams battle for the Grey Cup — Canadian football's highest trophy.

Lord Stanley

No Governor General's name is better known in Canada than that of Baron Stanley of Preston, our sixth Governor General (1888–1893). He was the son of a British Prime Minister and served in the British House of Commons before coming to Canada. To Canadians, though, he is the person who instituted the Stanley Cup for hockey excellence.

GOVERNORS GENERAL OF CANADA 1867–1995

The Viscount Monck
1867–1868

Lord Lisgar
1868–1872

The Earl of Dufferin
1872–1878

The Marquess of Lorne
1878–1883

The Marquess of Lansdowne
1883–1888

Lord Stanley
1888–1893

The Earl of Aberdeen
1893–1898

The Earl of Minto
1898–1904

Earl Grey
1904–1911

H.R.H. The Duke of Connaught
1911–1916

The Duke of Devonshire
1916–1921

Lord Byng of Vimy
1921–1926

The Viscount Willingdon
1926–1931

The Earl of Bessborough
1931–1935

Lord Tweedsmuir
1935–1940

The Earl of Athlone
1940–1946

The Viscount Alexander
1946–1952

Vincent Massey
1952–1959

George-P. Vanier
1959–1967

Roland Michener
1967–1974

Jules Léger
1974–1979

Edward Schreyer
1979–1984

Jeanne Sauvé
1984–1990

Ramon John Hnatyshyn
1990–1995

Roméo LeBlanc
1995–

The House of Commons

THE HOUSE OF Commons is the second element in our parliamentary system.

In the House of Commons, the elected representatives of all Canada's regions (called Members of Parliament or MPs) meet to debate and pass proposed laws, and to discuss issues of local, regional and national importance. The result is often a public clash of proposals and personalities, as MPs fight for what they feel is best for their constituency and their region.

To keep order in this place of strong feelings and opinions, the House of Commons is governed by rules of procedure called the Standing Orders. The House is also overseen by the Speaker, a Member of Parliament whose job it is to protect the rights of all Members and to discipline those who abuse these rights. As many of you know from watching the House of Commons on television, Members have sometimes made it a bitter and mean place. Some degree of anger or emotion is expected — after all, the important decisions made here affect our everyday lives. But the House should also be a place of dignity and courtesy, where mutual respect is practiced. Otherwise, the credibility of all MPs and the political process itself suffers.

Addressing Members of Parliament

In the House of Commons, MPs are normally referred to by the riding they represent, not by their first or family names. This tradition is meant to ensure that MPs treat each other and the Speaker with respect. An MP is therefore addressed as (for instance) "The Honourable Member for Ottawa Centre." The present and former Prime Ministers are called "The Right Honourable."

What's in a Name?

An MP who has been insulting or refuses to listen when told to do so by the Speaker is punished by being "named." This means that the Member is referred to by his or her own last name, rather than as the "Honourable Member for...(his or her riding's name)." The Member is then removed from the House of Commons chamber by the Sergeant-at-Arms. (This officer has been directed to remove the Member by the Speaker, or by a motion moved by the government House Leader and supported by a majority of the Members.) The MP can be suspended for as long as the House decides — one day or longer.

Some of you may have met your local Member of Parliament when he or she visited your area or when you were in Ottawa. Maybe you or your parents have worked on a candidate's election campaign. The private Member of Parliament is one of the most important people in our democratic system. He or she is the voice of individual Canadians in our only truly national forum — the elected House of Commons.

In 1988, I ran unsuccessfully for the House of Commons. I did this because I believed that the House of Commons needed more women, and Members who knew and understood Parliament. It was a way for me to serve my community and my country; and to use my education and experience to help others. We are very lucky in Canada and I believe that we all have a responsibility to ensure that Canada remains strong and united for our children to enjoy. Often you will hear arguments that a company president or union leader or some other powerful woman or man has more influence than Members of Parliament, and that may be true. But the House of Commons remains the only forum in our country where the problems of every Canadian — even those without power and influence — can be heard.

There have been many times when individual Canadians have had their problems resolved because of their local MP. In the early 1970s, for instance, I can remember a government "computer error" that stole the social insurance number of a young man from Burlington, Ontario. In effect, this removed his right to work, to receive pensions and to be eligible for government programs. Because the law at that time said a person could have only one social insurance number during his or her lifetime, he was refused a new number to replace the lost one. The department the poor man was dealing with told him to change his name — in effect become another person — and then maybe they could give him another number.

It could have been a modern-day nightmare, with a computer winning and a human being losing. But this man's Member of Parliament pursued the issue, worked to change the law about social insurance numbers, and helped the citizen prevail. This is but one of the countless examples of private Members of Parliament who go to bat for their constituents and work to make the system better.

I have never sat in the House of Commons, but I know many men and women who have. A few MPs might be accused of abusing the system or neglecting their duties as Members. But they are the exception. Nearly all Members of Parliament are hardworking, honest people. They have decided, as concerned and capable Canadians, to accept one of the responsibilities of democracy and to stand for public office.

Where's "Another Place"?

In Canada's system of Parliament, with its two Houses (the House of Commons and the Senate), a Member of the House of Commons may not refer to the proceedings of the Senate, and vice versa. To get around this rule, Members today refer to "another place" when talking of the other chamber. (When I first heard that term, I thought they were talking about Heaven!)

Please Do Not Adjust Your Set

Before there was television in the House, Members of Parliament indicated their approval by "rapping" or pounding on their desks with the palms of their hands. Enough television viewers objected to the tradition to make parliamentarians begin to applaud in the normal way by clapping their hands together. Applause by strangers seated in any of the galleries during regular sessions of the House of Commons is still not permitted. If you applaud, the security guard will ask you to stop or even to leave the chamber.

WHAT DO
MPs DO?

Many young people ask me, "What does an MP do each day?" Think of the MP's job as involving "the three Cs": the *constituency* (also called a "riding" — the area an MP represents), the *Commons* and the *committees*. The three are different, but equally important.

Constituency

Solving constituency problems is the most direct way an MP works for individual Canadians. Each MP has an office in Ottawa and may also have one in the constituency. There is a staff budget allocated to MPs to help them answer questions and deal with problems raised by individual constituents. For instance, constituents might have problems with unemployment insurance or pension rights or any other matter over which the federal government has control. Most MPs also work closely with the provincial members of the Legislature who represent their area. A federal constituency is much larger than a provincial one. This often means that one federal MP will work with as many as six provincial Members representing parts of his or her federal constituency in the provincial Legislature.

Here are some ways MPs serve their constituents:

☞ by holding meetings for constituents in the constituency to discuss matters of importance to them;

☞ by answering letters and phone calls from constituents and ensuring that their problems are solved;

☞ by introducing proposals in the House of Commons to change laws that hurt or affect their constituents;

☞ by speaking out (perhaps on television, radio or in the newspapers) to make people across Canada aware of the problems that exist in their region.

Many federal ridings are very large, especially in the northern parts of Canada. Rural MPs, in particular, often serve huge constituencies and cannot always be in every village and town. That is why it is important that you call or write your Member of Parliament if you have a problem. Your MP cannot read your mind. If you need help, you should ask for it. MPs' names are listed in the local phone books, and you can call a riding office without charge. Your MP will be happy to help you in any way possible.

Members of Parliament also have political party responsibilities — especially if they are well known. They must give speeches to organizations on all kinds of issues. They may also have to give political speeches in other Members' ridings to help them when they are seeking re-election or having special events such as fund-raising dinners or political conferences.

A Day in the Life of the House of Commons

Let us choose a Wednesday...

10:00 a.m.   *Party **caucuses** are held each Wednesday morning to bring all the members of the same political Party together in private to discuss current issues, political concerns, and the approaches they will take, as a Party, to the business of Parliament for that week. It is an important opportunity for MPs to bring up questions about Party and legislative policy, and to keep in touch with new issues facing Canadians.*

1:00 p.m.   *Lunch*

2:00 p.m.   ***Daily business** of the House of Commons begins.*

2:00 p.m.   ***Members' Statements** allows private Members of Parliament*
– 2:15 p.m.   *to make a one-minute statement on a matter of importance to the whole country or to the people living in their own constituency.*

2:15 p.m.   ***Question Period** is the part of the House of Commons proceedings*
– 3:00 p.m   *that most Canadians have seen on their televisions at night. It begins with an oral question to the Prime Minister or the senior Cabinet Minister designated as the "Acting Prime Minister" for that day. This question is usually "put" by the Leader of Her Majesty's Loyal Opposition or a senior MP in the Party with the second largest number of parliamentary seats. The questions then rotate through to other MPs, who have been designated to ask them because they have special knowledge of the issues (and may be their Party's "critic" on the area, such as the environment or health), or have asked for the opportunity to do so.*

3:00 p.m.   ***Routine Proceedings** follow the daily oral Question Period. It*
– 7:00 p.m.   *includes many things of a "housekeeping" nature, such as the tabling of documents, statements by Cabinet Ministers, the presentation of*

petitions MPs have collected, the presentation of Committee reports, the introduction and first reading of bills and debates of specific motions.

Notice of Motions for the Production of Papers *follows Routine Proceedings and allows MPs the chance to have their requests of the government for certain important papers to be granted. This only happens on Wednesdays.*

The proceedings end with ***Government Orders****, where any other items of business, including government motions, bills or questions, are placed on the House's agenda as Government Orders.*

7:00 p.m. – 8:00 p.m.   *Wednesday ends with* ***Private Members' Business****, where any MP who is not in Cabinet can present bills and motions for debate during this hour. It is another way to have issues brought before the House for discussion, although private Members' bills rarely become law.*

Ever wonder why your MP is not always on T.V. when you watch Parliament's proceedings in the House of Commons? Remember that Committee meetings can go on while the House of Commons is sitting; and they are not all held in Canada's capital, Ottawa. Special committees can travel across Canada, (and even to other countries) for meetings and public hearings, to inform MPs and Senators about a particular issue. Your MP works for you in many different ways, but especially in Parliament.

Former House of Commons Speaker Hon. John Fraser has written a book entitled: *The House of Commons at Work,* which describes the House of Commons' operation, structure and services. It is available for $19.95 in government bookstores across Canada. Refer to ISBN 2-89310-164-X.

Commons

When Canadians think about what Members of Parliament do, they usually visualize them in the House of Commons. We watch Question Period and debates on television, and we often see MPs asking or answering questions in the House of Commons. "House work" is an essential part of every Member of Parliament's day. The House of Commons is the stage upon which your Member of Parliament can make your views and concerns known to other MPs and — through the media — to the whole country. In the Commons, your MP can ask questions of Cabinet Ministers, make a statement on a local or national concern, debate proposed laws (called bills) the government has introduced, introduce a bill, make speeches on any matter and watch over how your tax money is spent. In the House of Commons, your MP becomes your eyes and ears, ensuring that the government takes into account the needs of all of Canada when laws are passed and important decisions are made.

The Commons can also be a frustrating place for a Member of Parliament. Television has brought with it a certain need for MPs to perform, almost like actors. When constituents do not see their Member on television, they sometimes think their MP is playing hookey. Because time is limited, only so many Members can ask questions each day of the Prime Minister and Cabinet Ministers. While the television camera is focused on Cabinet Ministers, there are many other Members whom you do not see. Except during Question Period, Committee meetings are going on at the same time as the debate in the House of Commons, so that as much detailed parliamentary work as possible can be done.

Rules of Question Period

When a Member asks a question during Question Period, the following guidelines apply. The question should:

- ☞ *be a question;*
- ☞ *be brief;*
- ☞ *seek information;*
- ☞ *address itself to an important matter of some urgency;*
- ☞ *be within the responsibility of the government or Minister questioned.*

It should not:

- ☞ *be a statement, representation, argument or expression of personal opinion;*
- ☞ *be hypothetical (that is, be about events that have not happened);*
- ☞ *seek an opinion from the Minister being questioned;*
- ☞ *suggest an answer;*
- ☞ *deal with a previous portfolio held by the Minister questioned;*

- *already have been answered that day;*
- *deal with a matter being considered by the courts (called* sub judice*);*
- *refer to statements or speeches made by Ministers outside the House;*
- *anticipate the matters to be dealt with later in the day.*

The Minister questioned may:
- *answer briefly;*
- *take the question as notice and answer on another day when he or she has had a chance to check the details involved;*
- *say nothing.*

Watch the Question Period on television one day. How many times do Members asking questions break one of the rules? What about the Ministers' answers?

Committees

While most Canadians at some point have watched the House of Commons proceedings on television, few know anything about the work of parliamentary committees. What you see on television is, in fact, only a small part of your MP's parliamentary duties. The detailed work is done in smaller groups of MPs called committees. Each party with elected MPs is represented. Committees allow MPs to divide the work and to specialize in certain areas that interest them. For instance, a farmer might want to serve on the Agriculture committee or a lawyer on the Justice committee.

To give the private member more power in Parliament's decision-making process, new rules were introduced in June 1985 to give Standing committees permanent Orders of Reference. They allow Standing committees to start their own investigations, instead of just dealing with matters that the House of Commons directs them to consider. Under the new rules, the chairpersons of these committees have a role that is, in many ways, as important and powerful as that of Parliamentary Secretaries. (See p. 47 for a discussion of Parliamentary Secretaries.)

There are now five major types of parliamentary committees:

☞ Standing (permanent) committees that are appointed for the life of a Parliament (up to five years). Their job is to consider all matters referred to them by the House of Commons and to report back to the MPs with their findings. Under the new rules, Standing committees can now start their own investigations as well.

☞ Legislative committees, which deal with bills referred to them after second reading in the House of Commons. These committees cease to exist when they have reported back to MPs on the bill they were studying.

☞ Special committees, which are appointed by the Commons to study specific matters. Sometimes they are called *task forces*.

☞ Joint committees, which are made up of both MPs and Senators. Some are Standing (permanent) and some are Special (for a specific purpose).

☞ Committees of the Whole, which occur when the House of Commons sits as a committee, and all the MPs are members of that committee. This rarely happens now.

Canada's is a system of responsible, not representative, government. This means that MPs owe more than blind allegiance to those who elected them. They are elected to be trail blazers and leaders as well as representatives of their own local interests. MPs are expected to use their experience, judgement and intelligence when contributing to debate and making important decisions. Sometimes these decisions will be based on personal or religious beliefs. These occasions are rare and are called *votes of conscience.* On such votes, MPs need not follow the party leader but may vote as they see fit.

You may not agree with all of your MP's decisions, and it is important that you let your MP know this. But one of the strengths of our system of government is that we elect human beings, not robots, to public office. If we have chosen well, then we will all be better off for the experience, integrity, intelligence and judgement an MP will bring to Parliament on our behalf. If not, then it is our responsibility and democratic right to choose another and better person in the following general election.

MPs Come in Pairs

If a Member has to be absent from the House of Commons, he or she agrees with a Member from another party to be absent at the same time. This is called "pairing." When Members are paired in this way, they cancel each other out if a vote is called while they are away.

The Maiden Speech

A Member's first speech in the House of Commons is called his or her "maiden speech." This first speech can be made at any time following the swearing-in of the Member. There have been Members who have never made a maiden speech during their entire time in the House of Commons!

HOW IS THE
GOVERNMENT
CHOSEN?

The political party that elects the most candidates at a general election is asked by the Governor General to form a government. If that political party has elected MPs in more than half the total number of constituencies, it forms what is called a *majority government*. This means that the government has enough members to pass the legislation it wants to introduce. It does not need to worry about being defeated on any vote, even if the opposition parties combined to vote against the government.

When the government does not have a clear majority, it forms a *minority government*. In this case, the opposition parties can join together at any time to vote against the government on any matter. In a parliamentary democracy, the government must be able to "command the confidence" of a majority of the MPs in the House of Commons. This means it must always have enough MPs in the House of Commons to carry every motion it introduces. If a minority government is defeated on an important vote (such as a budget) or on a vote that the government itself has said it considers to be a "matter of confidence," the government must resign. The Prime Minister must then ask the Governor General either to choose another Prime Minister or to call a general election.

43

Bouge? Budge? Budget?

The word "budget" is used to describe the government's financial plans for the year. It is said to come from the word "budge," an English form of the obsolete (not used any more) French word "bouge." Bouge meant "a small bag." The term "budget" was first used in the eighteenth century, in an English political cartoon. The Prime Minister — who also controlled the country's finances — was shown as a quack doctor explaining his financial measures by opening a bag full of useless medicines and charms. No doubt he was trying to lure an unsuspecting public into paying higher taxes!

WHO BECOMES
PRIME MINISTER?

In our parliamentary system, the leader of the political party with the largest number of elected Members of Parliament is asked by the Governor General to become the Prime Minister. The Prime Minister is referred to as "first among equals." In reality, the Prime Minister has much more power and influence than other Cabinet Ministers. For instance, the PM alone decides who will be in the Cabinet, and choses Parliamentary Secretaries and committee chairpersons. The PM has control over the more than 3,000 order-in-council appointments that can be made by the federal government. These are appointments of people to serve on federal boards and agencies, such as the CBC, the Canada Council and Air Canada. Under new rules, though, all order-in-council appointments (except judges) can be reviewed by a parliamentary committee.

THE
CABINET

The Cabinet is the group of Members of Parliament (and sometimes Senators) who are responsible for deciding the Government's policies and plans. They are normally chosen from among all the MPs elected for the same political party as the Prime Minister. Usually, each province is represented by at least one Cabinet Minister. In exceptional circumstances — for instance, if the government has not elected any Members of Parliament for a certain province — a Senator may also be named to the Cabinet. It is very important that all regions be represented, because it is Cabinet that decides what plans the government will follow. Each region should have a voice in these decisions.

A person could be appointed to Cabinet even if he or she were not an MP or Senator. However, that person would have to be elected or named a Senator as soon as possible after the appointment. Otherwise, the Cabinet Minister could not sit in Parliament. He or she would have to arrange for someone else to answer questions in Question Period. Remember, even a Senator is not able to sit in the House of Commons, but would be asked questions in the Senate by other members of the Senate.

Each Cabinet Minister is a Member of Parliament (or Senator) and is appointed by the Prime Minister to be responsible for a certain policy area, such as Foreign Affairs, Finance, Health or Justice. This area of responsibility is called the Minister's "portfolio." A Minister is responsible to the people, through Parliament, for all the activities that take place within that portfolio. In complex and senior departments, Cabinet Ministers may have other Ministers working under them. For instance, the Minister of Foreign Affairs is responsible for all aspects of Canada's foreign policy. But today, other Ministers have been asked to assume responsibility for specific parts of the world and for particular issues of international importance to Canada, such as trade and foreign aid. The Department of Foreign Affairs in Ottawa and our diplomats around the world work with these Ministers to ensure that Canada's interests are professionally and well represented in every major country, as well as every international organization or group of which Canada is a member. Some of these are the United Nations, NATO, the G–7 and the Commonwealth.

A Member of Parliament can also be named a Minister without Portfolio. This means that, although the person is a Cabinet Minister, he or she does not have any specific "portfolio." Such a person will usually be asked to carry out special assignments, either for the Prime Minister or for a senior Minister with a very complex and important portfolio.

Parliamentary Secretaries are also Members of Parliament and are often described as "Cabinet Ministers-in-training." Their responsibilities include answering questions in the House of Commons when the Minister is away, giving speeches and attending functions when the Minister cannot do so. This division of work allows very busy Ministers to give more time and consideration to other important matters.

Parliamentary Firsts for Women

☞ Agnes Campbell Macphail was the first woman to be elected to the House of Commons. She was elected in 1921 as a member of the Progressive Party, from the Ontario riding of Grey South East.

☞ Ellen Fairclough was the first woman Cabinet Minister. She was first elected as a Progressive Conservative member for the Ontario riding of Hamilton West in 1950. Named Secretary of State by Prime Minister Diefenbaker in 1957, she later served as Minister of Citizenship and Immigration and Postmaster General.

☞ Jeanne Sauvé was the first woman Speaker of the House of Commons, from 1980 to 1984. She then served as Canada's Governor General from 1984 to 1989 — another first for Canadian women.

☞ Cairine R. Wilson was the first woman appointed to the Senate, in February 1930.

☞ Mariana B. Jodouin was the first French-Canadian woman summoned to the Senate. She served from 1953 to 1966.

- Muriel Fergusson, from Shediac, New Brunswick, was the first woman to be named Speaker of the Senate. She was appointed to the Senate in 1953 and served as its Speaker from 1972 to 1974.
- Renaude Lapointe was the first French-Canadian woman Speaker of the Senate, from 1974 to 1979.
- Flora MacDonald, former MP for Kingston and the Islands in Ontario, was the first woman, in 1979, to serve as Canada's Foreign Minister. Barbara McDougall assumed the same role in 1993.
- Mary Collins, MP from Vancouver, British Columbia, became the first woman Defence Minister in 1991.
- Kim Campbell, from Vancouver, British Columbia, became Canada's first woman Prime Minister in June 1993, when she was elected leader of the Progressive Conservative Party to replace then-Prime Minister Brian Mulroney.
- Sheila Copps, long-time MP from Hamilton, Ontario, was named the first woman Deputy Prime Minister after the 1993 federal election.

THE OFFICIAL OPPOSITION

The political party that elects the second largest number of Members of Parliament forms the official Opposition. Their party leader becomes the Leader of Her Majesty's Loyal Opposition.

The Leader of the Opposition could also be described as a Prime Minister-in-waiting. Among other things, the Leader of the Opposition's responsibilities include:

☞ criticizing government proposals;

☞ suggesting ways that the government's legislation can be improved; and

☞ putting forth his or her own party's ideas about how it would proceed if it formed the government after the next federal election.

Canadians can then decide which party leader they think would be the best person to serve as Prime Minister after the next federal election.

For the first time ever, in 1993 Her Majesty's Loyal Opposition was represented by a political party whose goal was to have one province, Quebec, leave Canada to form another independent country. Neither this party, called the Bloc Québécois, nor the third opposition party, called the Reform Party, elected MPs outside their provinces or region.

THE SHADOW CABINET

The Leader of the official Opposition names a group of Members of Parliament to form a "shadow cabinet." These MPs have the special duty each day of asking Ministers questions in the House of Commons. They must also comment and make speeches on certain bills and government proposals that fall within their special areas. For instance, the shadow minister for the Agricultural portfolio would be responsible for asking the Minister of Agriculture all farm-related questions. This shadow minister would usually be the first Member of the Opposition to speak on any agricultural legislation that the Government was proposing.

Often, both Cabinet Ministers and shadow cabinet ministers are people with special expertise in a given area.

For instance, a farmer may become Minister of Agriculture, a lawyer may become the Minister of Justice or the Solicitor General, and an economist or accountant may become the Minister of Finance.

OTHER
OPPOSITION
PARTIES

All other political parties who have members elected to the House of Commons are referred to simply as the opposition. Their leaders have the first opportunity, after the Leader of the official Opposition, to ask questions during Question Period. The number of questions allowed each opposition party is based on the number of seats they won in the last general election. The number of seats a party represents in Parliament is referred to as their "standing" in the House of Commons.

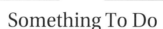

Something To Do

Help with Your Homework

Did you know that federal government departments publish many free articles and booklets each year that could help you with reports and essays for school?

Here are some suggestions on what to do after you have chosen your topic:

☞ Each government department has a communications or public affairs section. They have lists of all the documents that have been published and released by their department. Write them or call the number listed in your local phone book.

(Government numbers are in the blue pages at the back of the phone book.)

☞ You can also write to your MP or the Cabinet Minister responsible for your research area. Both would provide you with the material that is available. Remember to be as specific as possible about what you need, and to write well in advance of your deadline. *However, don't expect them to actually write your essay for you!*

In Parliament, there are two Speakers — one for the elected House of Commons and one for the appointed Senate. The Speakers have one of the hardest jobs on Parliament Hill. Using a sports analogy, the Speaker is like a referee or umpire. MPs may not agree with the Speaker's ruling, but they must follow it. The Speaker is there to ensure that the rights of all parliamentarians are respected. Like a referee, the Speaker must be impartial (must not take sides).

This impartiality is particularly important in Canada. Unlike Britain, the Speaker of the House of Commons is a Member of Parliament who has been elected as a candidate for one of the major political parties. The Speaker of the Senate is appointed by the Prime Minister.

The name "Speaker" is actually a little misleading, since the Speaker does not take part in debates in the House of Commons. Neither can the Speaker vote on a bill, except where there is a tie. Then the Speaker must cast the deciding vote. Although the Speaker of the Senate can take part in debate on matters before that chamber, it is now the custom that he or she does not. This helps the Speaker appear less partisan (*Partisan* means supporting one group or side over another).

THE SPEAKER OF THE HOUSE OF COMMONS

A new Speaker is elected from among all of the Members of Parliament in the House of Commons after each federal election. Until recently, the Speaker was actually chosen by the Prime Minister. When Members of Parliament voted to elect the Speaker, they were in fact endorsing (accepting or approving) the Prime Minister's choice. The Leader of the Opposition usually seconded (suported) the motion that the Prime Minister's choice of Speaker be accepted.

Before 1986, the Speaker was appointed by the Prime Minister. Now, a more democratic procedure is in place. The Speaker is elected by her/his peers in the House of Commons.

The procedure is quite simple. Any MP, except Cabinet Ministers and party leaders, can be a candidate for the position of Speaker. The MPs then vote, by secret ballot, and the candidate with the majority of votes becomes the Speaker.

The Speaker must make difficult, often controversial, rulings every day, on behalf of all the parties in the House of Commons. Tempers flare and MPs often disagree on many issues. If Members do not respect and listen to the Speaker, then the work of Parliament and the conduct of its affairs is badly affected. An elected Speaker has more authority to make the tough decisions — even when, in the end, the decision may not be the one all of the MPs would have preferred.

Under this new system, the Speaker's authority really does flow from the other MPs in the House of Commons.

WHAT DOES THE SPEAKER DO?

The Speaker's main duties include:
- ☞ Presiding daily over the debates and proceedings of the House of Commons.
- ☞ Representing the House of Commons in all its external relations. For instance, the Speaker must receive and entertain all Members of Parliament or representatives of foreign countries who come to Canada. The Speaker must also lead delegations of Canadian parliamentarians abroad.

- Being responsible, along with the Speaker of the Senate, for all Members' facilities, such as the Library of Parliament and the parliamentary restaurants.
- Participating in all of the traditional ceremonies of Parliament, such as the daily Speaker's Parade to the House of Commons, and attending the Senate to hear Royal Assent being given to all bills passed by both Houses.
* The Speaker is no longer responsible for the House of Commons budget. Pursuant to s. 52.3 of *The Parliament of Canada Act,* the Speaker is Chairman of the Board of Internal Economy, which has been responsible for the budget since the mid–1980s. The House of Commons budget for 1994–95 was $238,450,000.

Want to see the Speaker at work? Join two students as they prepare a video for a school project. Copies of the video "Inside Parliament: The Speakership" (26 min.) are available from the Public Information Office of the House of Commons, Ottawa, Canada, K1A 0A4.

The Speaker's Chair

The original Speaker's chair was destroyed in the great fire in 1916. The one used now was given to Canada on May 20, 1921, by a branch of the Empire Parliamentary Association. It was an exact replica of the Speaker's chair in the British House of Commons. (The British chair was itself destroyed in 1941 during a World War II air raid over London.) The Royal Coat of Arms in the canopy above the Canadian

Commons Speaker's chair is carved from a piece of oak almost 600 years old, taken from the roof of Westminster Hall in England. As a sign of respect, all Members of Parliament bow in the direction of the Speaker when passing in front of the Speaker's chair and when entering or leaving the Commons chamber.

THE CLERK OF THE HOUSE OF COMMONS

The Clerk of the House of Commons is like the Speaker's right hand. The Clerk sits at the table in front of the Speaker, with a Clerk Assistant at either side. Among other administrative duties, the Clerk assists the Speaker and Members on all questions of parliamentary procedure; certifies and audits all the accounts of the House of Commons; and administers the oath of allegiance to newly elected Members.

The Clerk's Chair

After Confederation, when the Clerk of the House of Commons left his job, he took with him the chair he had occupied on the floor of the House of Commons. This custom is no longer followed. The chair now used by the Clerk belonged to Sir John C. Bourniot, Clerk of the House of Commons between 1880 and 1903. His son offered it to the House of Commons in his father's memory.

What's the Mace?

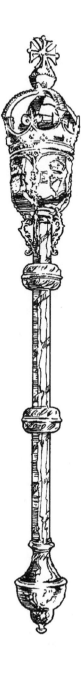

The Mace was first used in England by King Richard I, whose bodyguards — the Sergeants-at-Arms — carried them for his protection. Even before that, heavy maces made of iron were carried by the bishops (high ranking clergymen) into battle. By the religious laws of the time, bishops could not use a weapon like a sword that would draw blood. (I imagine the mace left a rather large dent in the other fellow's head, though!)

Today, the Mace is a large, gold, ornamented club that symbolizes the ancient authority of the Crown, now exercised by Parliament. It is carried in the Speaker's Parade by the Sergeant-at-Arms. The Mace is on the table on the floor of the House of Commons when the Speaker is in the chair, and on brackets underneath the table when he or she is out of the chamber. It is a long-standing tradition that the House cannot legally sit without the Mace on the table. (The same applies for the Senate Mace.)

The present Mace in the House of Commons is a replacement for the one lost in the 1916 fire. A portion of the old Mace was recovered from the ashes, and made part of the new one. This Mace is a copy of the one in the British House of Commons, and was a gift from the Sheriffs of London, England.

THE
SERGEANT-
AT-ARMS

The Sergeant-at-Arms is like a police officer and is usually a person with a military background. Duties are both ceremonial (for show) and substantive (for a real purpose). As part of the security duties, the Sergeant-at-Arms hires employees such as constables, messengers and other employees of the House of Commons as they are needed. The Sergeant-at-Arms also accompanies the Speaker of the House of Commons when the Speaker is carrying out his or her official parliamentary duties.

PAGES

The young men and women you see on televison sitting at the foot of the Speaker's chair are pages. They are university students who act as messengers to MPs and the Speaker.

Something To Do

Student Jobs in Parliament

Have you ever thought of working on Parliament Hill as a page, a parliamentary guide, or even in an MP or Minister's office? When I was at university, I pursued my interest in politics and the law by working on special research projects during the summer, and helping out with constituency questions and problems after classes during the school year. It is a super way to make new friends and contacts, and to gain experience for future jobs.

For more information on the page and parliamentary guide programs for the House of Commons, write to:

Education and Visitors Services
Public Information Office
House of Commons
Ottawa, Canada, K1A OA6
(613) 995-4416

Citizenship Programs

Thousands of young Canadians can take advantage of special programs aimed at helping them develop a respect and understanding of their responsibilities as Canadian citizens. Here are some of the organizations which work with Parliament to bring young Canadians to our nation's capital to see for themselves how Parliament works.

✦✦ *Adventure in Citizenship* ✦✦

Operated by the Rotary Club for many years, this program still draws many young Canadians to Ottawa to see Parliament first-hand. It was, for instance, as a result of his trip to Ottawa as a "Young Adventurer" that my husband, Joe Clark, began a lifelong interest in Parliament, where he served in many senior positions for over two decades. Contact your local Rotary Club, or write to the Ottawa Host Club at the Chateau Laurier, Ottawa, Canada, K1N 8S7.

✦✦ *Forum for Young Canadians* ✦✦

If you can spare a full week between March and May, try to come to Ottawa to one of the four sessions sponsored by the Forum for Young Canadians. You might be lucky enough to see the annual Tulip Festival, which marks the return of Spring and the role Ottawa played as the home of the Dutch Royal Family during World War II. At the Forum, senior parliamentarians from all parties take time out of their busy schedules to speak directly to the young Canadians, who come from across the country to learn about consensus-building and working together to solve tough national problems. Talk to your MP, school principal, or write to the Forum offices at 251 Laurier Ave. W., Suite 801, Ottawa, Canada, K1P 5J6.

✦✦ *The Terry Fox Canadian Youth Centre* ✦✦

Most of us will never forget the pictures of Terry Fox, the young man who decided to run across Canada to raise awareness of cancer — the disease which robbed him of one leg and later killed him. The effort and dedication of this young high school student took on heroic proportions, and his name has become synonymous with courage and victory over pain. His short life, and the values he represented and encouraged in all of us, spawned the Encounters with Canada program, offered to high school students for one week in Ottawa. Write to: The Terry Fox Canadian Youth Centre, P.O. Box 7279, Ottawa, Canada, K1L 8E3.

◆◆ *The 4-H Citizenship Seminar* ◆◆

Like many people who grew up in the country, I was an active member of the 4-H clubs in my part of eastern Ontario. If you are also a member of 4-H, and want to see Ottawa for a week with other 4-H members from rural communities across Canada, speak to your 4-H leader, or write to the Canadian 4-H Council, 1690 Woodward Drive, Suite 208, Ottawa, Canada, K2C 3R8.

◆◆ *Parliamentary Internship* ◆◆

Older students who have completed university or are at graduate school have the chance to work for a year, as a research and political assistant to a Minister or member of one or more parties. Sponsored by the Canadian Political Science Association, this intensive program also includes a trip to Washington to see the American legislative process in action. Write to the Parliamentary Internship Program at 205 - 1 Stewart St., Ottawa, Canada, K1N 6H7.

◆◆ *Canadian Opportunities Student Employment Program (COSEP)* ◆◆

While at university, students from across Canada are invited to apply to work with the COSEP program during the four summer months. This is an excellent opportunity to work in the federal Public Service, and to make valuable contacts and new friends. Ask for the application form from the Employment Office on your university or college campus. If you were active in politics as a youth worker, contact your MP to see if she/he will support your application with a letter of reference.

✦✦ *Work for your MP in Ottawa or in the Riding Offices* ✦✦

You may also want to volunteer to work in your MP's constituency or parliamentary office, to gain experience and help out. Most MPs can always use intelligent and eager students to research answers for constituents' questions, draft correspondence, arrange riding tours, prepare their quarterly mailing (called a "householder," because it is sent to every household in the constituency) and many, many other tasks. Remember, while it is always nice to be paid, voluntarism is also part of our civic duty; and many young people — myself included — started by volunteering to help out on political campaigns and in MPs' offices. The experience you will acquire will be worth its weight in gold, and you will also be contributing personally to making Canada's parliamentary system work.

🍁

Learn About Our History and Citizenship

Many government-sponsored programs encourage a better understanding of Canada's history. Learn more about Canadian citizenship, our linguistic duality, multicultural heritage, and Aboriginal peoples by writing to:

Communications Branch
Multiculturalism & Citizenship Canada
Ottawa, Canada
K1A OK5

🍁

The Senate

THE THIRD ELEMENT of our parliamentary system is the Senate. When Canada became a country in 1867, the Senate was a very important part of Confederation. Since representation by population was used in the House of Commons, the regions with fewer people (Quebec and the Maritimes) worried that their voices would not be heard. They wanted a Senate in which each region would have equal representation. The Senate today has 104 members: six from Newfoundland, 24 from the three Maritime provinces, 24 from Quebec, 24 from Ontario, 24 from the four Western provinces, and one each from the Yukon and Northwest Territories.

WHO CAN BECOME A SENATOR?

To qualify for the Senate, a person must:
☞ be a citizen of Canada;
☞ be at least 30 years of age;
☞ own at least $4,000 worth of real property (for instance, land, a building, a home) within the province for which he or she is appointed; and
☞ be a resident of that province.

In addition, in Quebec Senators must either own land or live in the electoral division for which they are appointed.

Generally, a Senator can lose his or her seat:

☞ through death;
☞ upon reaching age 75 (if appointed after 1965);
☞ by missing two consecutive Sessions of Parliament;
☞ by becoming a citizen of another country;
☞ by becoming bankrupt or insolvent (unable to pay debts);
☞ by no longer owning real property or living in the district or province for which he or she is appointed; or
☞ by being convicted of an indictable offense under the Criminal Code (this would include treason, murder, robbery and other such serious crimes).

Emily Murphy • Henrietta Muir Edwards • Louise McKinney • Irene Parlby • Nellie McClung

Are Women "Persons"?

Does this seem like a ridiculous question to you? Well, only 60 years ago (about the time your grandparents were children), Canadian women had to fight to prove that they were, indeed, persons.

Section 24 of the British North America Act, 1867 *read:*

"The Governor General shall from time to time, in the Queen's name, by instrument under the Great Seal of Canada, summon qualified Persons to the Senate: and subject to the provisions of this Act, every Person so summoned shall become a member of the Senate and a Senator."

The Liberal government of Prime Minister Mackenzie King refused to appoint a woman to the Senate until the courts had settled the issue of whether women were "persons" under the BNA Act.

Five prominent Alberta women decided to take the question to the Supreme Court of Canada. They were Emily F. Murphy, a legal magistrate from Edmonton (who was the group's unofficial leader), Henrietta Muir Edwards from Macleod, Nellie L. McClung from Edmonton, Louise C. McKinney from Claresholm and the Honourable Irene Parlby from Alix.

The question to be decided was: "Does the word 'person' in Section 24 of the British North America Act, 1867, *include 'female persons'?" The judges of the Supreme Court of Canada said No. Undaunted, the Famous Five (as they were later called), appealed the decision of the Supreme Court to the Judicial Committee of the Privy Council in England. Until 1949, this was Canada's highest court of appeal. Their victory at that court ensured that women were officially persons under their own Constitution.*

On Valentine's Day, February 14, 1930, Cairine R. Wilson of Ottawa was appointed as the first woman to the Canadian Senate.

Like MPs, Senators have various responsibilities and duties. First, a Senator is a legislator (a person who makes laws). The Senate has the same powers as the House of Commons to make laws, except that it cannot propose a law to raise or spend public money. Only the House of Commons, whose members are elected, can do this.

Second, a Senator should be a regional representative. In 1867, the role of the Senate was to speak up for regional interests that mattered to Canadians living in places away from Ottawa. Today, this special role for Senators is less important. The premiers, who represent their provinces and other regional interests, now meet regularly with the Prime Minister at conferences to discuss problems.

Third, Senators have an investigative role. The Senate was intended to be a place of "sober second thought." Here, Senators would have the time and the help to investigate problems and propose changes in a wise and careful manner. Because Senators are appointed, they are free from the pressures of re-election and have the time to study an issue completely, so that the correct answers can be found to solve serious national and regional problems. Senators do this regularly. On notable occasions — such as its report on Aging and the one on Children at Risk — the Senate has changed public policy.

SENATE
REFORM

Today, most Canadians question the need for a second Chamber, or Upper House, and challenge the Senate's legitimacy. Unlike MPs, who are elected by popular vote to serve during the life of a Parliament, Senators are appointed by the Governor General, and are chosen by the Prime Minister. Until 1965, they were appointed for life; they are now entitled to stay on until they are 75 years old.

Many people have proposed that the Senate be abolished. They see it as a place of patronage only, and do not believe that it serves any useful purpose in the legislative process. Recently, many people have been concerned that the real role of the Senate, as a place where government legislation can be studied, and even stopped, has been eliminated. They point to the 1990 decision by Prime Minister Mulroney to use an obscure constitutional provision, Section 26 of the *BNA Act, 1867*, to have eight new Senators appointed, thus increasing the total to 112. Many felt he did this to ensure that certain unpopular and controversial legislation which the Liberal Senators refused to support would be passed by the Senate, and become law.

Section 26 allows the Queen, on the recommendation of the Governor General (who acts on the advice of the Prime Minister) to direct that either 4 or 8 persons, from each of Canada's four regions, be named to the Senate. On September 27, 1990, the Queen agreed, and 8 new Senators were appointed. The Government's legislation passed.

This action was often cited, by critics of the Senate, as an example of its illegitimacy and uselessness. This led to several proposals for radical change to the Senate in the constitutional talks in 1992. In *The Charlottetown Accord,* the federal government, the ten provinces, the Northwest Territories and the Yukon, as well as all the participating Aboriginal Leaders, agreed to reform the Senate.

THE CHARLOTTETOWN ACCORD

The Charlottetown Accord proposed radical reform to the Senate, to make it elected and equal, and therefore a more legitimate and effective legislative body. (We'll be discussing the Accord's proposed changes in more detail later in the book.)

An Elected Senate

Under this Accord,

☞ *Senators would be elected, either by direct vote of the eligible people in each province and the territories of Canada, or by the members of their provincial or territorial legislative assemblies.*

☞ *The Elections Act would govern elections to the Senate, which would take place at the same time as general elections for the House of Commons.*

☞ *Provinces and the Territories would be able to provide for gender equality in the composition of the Senate.*

An Equal Senate

☞ *The Senate would initially total 62 Senators, with an option to add more Senators to represent each new province that might be created in the future.*

☞ *Ontario and Quebec gave up 18 Senate seats, so that all provinces would have six Senators each. Each Territory had one Senator.*

Aboriginal Senators

☞ *Aboriginal representation would be guaranteed in the Senate.*

☞ *Aboriginal Senate seats would be in addition to those allotted each province and Territory.*

☞ *Aboriginal Senators would have the same role and powers as other Senators. A "double majority" power was also discussed. This would require a majority of the Aboriginal Senators, as well as a majority of all Senators, to agree to certain legislation with a direct impact on Aboriginal rights.*

Categories of Legislation

There would be four categories of legislation in the Senate:

☞ *Revenue and expenditure bills ("Supply bills")*

☞ *Legislation materially affecting French language or culture*

☞ *Tax policy legislation*

☞ *Ordinary legislation*

Approval of Legislation

☞ *The Accord provided for certain new rules about approving legislation. To avoid delays, for instance, with the exception of money Bills, the Senate would be required by the Constitution to pass House of Commons Bills within 30 sitting days of their passage in the Commons.*

☞ *Bills materially affecting French language and culture would have to be passed by both a majority of Senators and a majority of francophone Senators voting. The House of Commons would not be able to override the defeat of this kind of Bill by the Senate.*

☞ *Where ordinary legislation was defeated or amended, the House of Commons and Senate would sit jointly, and a simple majority vote would decide the question.*

☞ *As before, the Senate could not initiate money Bills.*

Ratification of Appointments

☞ *The Senate would be given additional powers, including those to ratify key appointments made by the federal government, including the Governor of the Bank of Canada.*

The Charlottetown Accord was rejected in a national referendum vote in October 1992.

Until a new round of constitutional talks are undertaken in Canada, several things would help encourage greater confidence in the institution of the Senate. For example, Senators could agree to serve for a limited period of time — say seven years — instead of for life. This would fit with the principle that in a true democracy no unelected body should ever serve for life. The Prime Minister could agree to appoint people from a broader cross-section of Canadian life, and from among people who have already contributed significantly to their community and province.

Senators themselves could contribute to this process by insisting that the rules of conflict of interest that apply to Cabinet Ministers also apply to them. This would help reassure people that those enjoying the privileges and pay of public office are putting their parliamentary duties first and foremost.

Canadians should analyze in detail the many changes proposed by *The Charlottetown Accord,* to be ready for the next stage of constitutional reform, and to make the Senate an accountable, legitimate and modern part of our parliamentary democracy.

Something To Do

A Close-up of the Senate

Several booklets and pamphlets are available from the Senate free of charge. For your copies, write to:

    Senate Communications
    The Senate of Canada
    Ottawa, Canada, K1A 0A4
    (613) 992-1149

Check the blue pages in your local phone book for the Senate's toll-free number. Remember, no stamp is required on your letters to either an MP or Senator.

Students and teachers in primary grades wanting an adventure in Canada's Parliament should ask for a video resource package (also available in closed and open captioning for the hearing-impaired) prepared by the House of Commons Public Information Office. For further details, write to:

    The Education Officer
    House of Commons
    Ottawa, Canada, K1A OA6

The Legislative Process

I F ASKED WHAT Parliament does, most Canadians would reply that it passes laws. Few people, though, would know what that actually means. Under our Constitution, the federal and provincial governments can each pass laws in certain specified areas only. (We'll be looking at Canada's Constitution in more detail later in the book.)

WHAT IS A
BILL?

A bill is a written draft of a proposed law. It sets out a proposal for Parliament to consider in full. Parliament may then reject it, or approve it and pass it, with or without amendments (changes). There are several steps that must be taken when passing a bill into law. Taken together, these steps are called the *legislative process*.

There are two main types of bills — public bills and private bills. (We will only look here at public bills, since private bills are now rare.) As their name suggests, public bills relate to matters of public policy. Either they affect all Canadians or a particular group of Canadians. For instance, you could have a section of the *Income Tax Act* that affects all Canadians with children — such as the basic deduction given to parents and guardians for each child under a certain age who is in their care. You could also have, within the same Act, a section that affects only one group. For example, the *Income Tax Act* could have a section that gives special tax advantages to companies that set up business in areas where unemployment is high.

There are two kinds of public bills. There are those introduced by the government — usually through a Cabinet Minister — which are called *government bills.* There are also those introduced by private Members either of the government or the opposition. These are called *private Members' Public bills.*

If you look at *A Day in the Life of the House of Commons* on pp. 36–37, you will see that private Members' bills are given very limited time during which they can be debated and considered in Parliament. This is mainly because it is felt that Parliament's time is better spent on bills introduced by the government, which affect everyone in the country. Private Members' bills, though, do serve a useful purpose. They give an MP who is not a Minister the chance to make known his or her views on a subject. If this subject is controversial (likely to cause strong feelings for and against), the Member can usually count on some publicity in the press. This will help his or her cause, and may even bring public pressure on the government to consider the matter further.

What is a Motion?

Almost all parliamentary business is carried on by motion. Two exceptions are oral questions and Members' statements. A motion is like the start button on a machine. Watch the Speaker on television. Each time you hear the sentence "Moved by…seconded by…that…," you will know MPs are being asked to debate and make another decision. They can either call out their support (by saying "Aye!") or refuse it (by saying "Nay!"). The Speaker decides who wins. If five members refuse to accept the decision by rising in their places, there has to be a recorded vote. The Speaker says "call in the Members" and a recorded vote is taken. This is called a division — the House divides into those MPs who support the motion and those who do not.

This comes from the British tradition, where MPs actually leave the chamber and divide into two separate lobbies — one for those who support the motion and one for those against it. In Canada, the Members vote on a motion by rising in their place and bowing towards the Speaker.

HOW A BILL
BECOMES LAW

There are a number of basic steps through which a public bill must pass before becoming law. Some of these stages are called "readings." This term dates from the time in England when the Clerk actually read out each bill. This practice is not followed in Canada. MPs and Senators have to read the bills on their own before voting on them. Here is what happens to a public bill:

☞ The government gives a written notice to the Commons Clerk saying it plans to introduce a bill in two days. This is published in a daily publication called the *Notice Paper*, which is sent to all MPs each day that Parliament is in session.

☞ The Minister responsible introduces the bill in the House, and asks for it to be given *first reading* and to be printed. No debate (discussion) is allowed at this point. MPs either accept or reject the bill. If it is accepted, it is then printed and distributed to all MPs.

☞ One or two weeks later, the same Minister explains, in a speech in the House of Commons, the reasons for the bill. Opposition MPs reply in speeches. This debate on the motion for *second reading* of the bill is often called a debate on the principle of the bill (that is, the bill's main purpose).

☞ The bill goes to committee for detailed study. Amendments (changes) can be made to it by MPs at the *committee stage*.

☞ The committee's report is presented in the House of Commons by the committee chairperson.

☞ At the *report stage*, the House of Commons considers the bill and any amendments as reported by the committee. Events that took place in the committee can be reconsidered. Even amendments rejected by the committee can be reintroduced. The House then sets a date for *third reading*.

☞ At *third reading*, MPs have one last chance to review and vote on the bill in its final proposed form after all amendments have been added.

☞ The bill goes to the Senate for consideration. Basically, the same procedure followed in the House is repeated in the Senate.

☞ If the Senate makes any amendments, they are sent back to the House of Commons. MPs can accept, reject or amend the amendments proposed by the Senate.

☞ After all of the above is completed, the bill is ready for *Royal Assent*. A special ceremony is held in the Senate Chamber, attended by representatives of both Houses of Parliament and a representative of the Governor General. The titles of the bills are read out, and the Governor General's representative gives assent by nodding his or her head. Unless otherwise specified in the bill, it becomes law at this point. (Some bills set out a date on which they will become law.)

If you want to make your views known on any bill, you can write to your MP or a Senator who is serving on the committee studying the particular bill. You can also ask to present your views in writing (called a brief or representation), or you can go to a public hearing if one is being held in your area.

Filibustering

"Filibustering" is the name given to the tactics opposition parties use to stop the government from passing legislation. In the United States, this usually means speaking on and on just to use up time. Until June 1985, the opposition in Canada could ring the bells calling the Members to vote for an unlimited period. Since then, the House of Commons has amended its own Standing Orders to provide that the bells ring for only half an hour to call in the MPs before a vote. The opposition in Canada now tends to use other tactics to delay the passage of government legislation. For instance, MPs will rise and present hundreds of petitions, or force unnecessary votes in the House of Commons.

The Electoral Process

CONSTITUENCIES

At the federal level, Canada is divided into electoral areas known as *constituencies* or *ridings*. The boundaries are chosen so that, as much as possible, every MP has about the same number of constituents.

Parts of the country where there are more people have more Members of Parliament. This means that Quebec and Ontario, which have the largest populations, have the greatest number of Members of Parliament — 99 from Ontario and 75 from Quebec.

A city riding in Ontario, fairly small in area, could have almost 250,000 constituents, while the whole Yukon has less than 25,000. Members of Parliament who represent huge northern ridings receive extra money to help them cover the additional cost of serving such a large area. In a city riding, an MP could drive to meetings. In the big northern or rural ridings, though, an MP may have to rent a plane or helicopter just to be able to see constituents once a year.

Gerrymandering

The word "gerrymander" means to place the boundaries of constituencies in such a way as to give an unfair advantage to the party or politician in power. Apparently, a group of politicians were studying an electoral map in the United States in the nineteenth century. One of them commented on the unusual snakelike shape of the ridings, saying,

"It looks like a salamander." Another replied, "You mean a gerrymander!" He was referring to a well-known Massachusetts governor whose last name was Gerry and who used the practice of "gerrymandering" very effectively to protect his own political interests.

REDISTRIBUTION

Every ten years, the Canadian government counts how many people live in Canada. This is called the *Census*. The figures are used to re-adjust the boundaries and number of ridings in Canada. This process is called *redistribution*. Its goal is to keep the ridings about equal in the number of people they contain. It also takes into account population shifts from one part of Canada to another. Redistribution is handled through a special department called the Electoral Boundaries Commission, which is part of the Chief Electoral Officer's responsibility. The Chief Electoral Officer is a public servant who looks after all the requirements for holding federal elections.

🍁

Something To Do

Yours for the Asking

The Public Information Office of the House of Commons has designed several brochures and booklets to help you better understand how Parliament works. Here is a sample of some of the many resource materials, in English and in French, that are available for the asking.

☞ Guide to the House of Commons
☞ The Parliament Buildings
☞ The Memorial Chamber
☞ The House of Commons
☞ The Library of Parliament
☞ The Speaker
☞ Bringing the House to Canadian Homes: The House of Commons Broadcasting Service

Here are some Fact Sheets that you might want:

☞ On the Job with a Member of Parliament

☞ The Role of Cabinet
☞ Parliamentary Secretaries
☞ Youth Opportunities on Parliament Hill
☞ Canada's Story: The Road to Confederation & Beyond
☞ O Canada
☞ Canada's Coat of Arms
☞ Question Period
☞ Television in the House of Commons
☞ The Legislative Process
☞ Where to Get Information on Canada's Parliamentary System
☞ A Week in the House

Remember that you can also watch the *Proceedings of the House of Commons,* when Parliament is sitting, on the House of Commons Broadcasting channel. Check your local listings for the channel and times.

Political parties are the human organizations that make our system of government work. Anyone can join a political party. Each political party is made up of people who share similar ideas about the role and responsibilities of the individual and government.

After the 1993 election, Parliament looked radically different. The Progressive Conservative Party, which had been a majority government since September 1984, was decimated, and lost its standing as an official Party in the House of Commons. The New Democratic Party also lost seats, and became the third largest opposition party in the Commons.

A majority Liberal government replaced the Progressive Conservative one, with MPs elected in every province. For the first time in Canadian history, the official Opposition, the Bloc Québécois, was a party whose members were elected exclusively from Quebec, and who were dedicated to the separation of Quebec from Canada. Another new political party, the Reform Party, formed the second opposition party. Like the official Opposition, the Reform Party was regionally based, and did not run candidates in all of the ridings across Canada. All but one of its elected MPs were from Western Canada.

Where Do You Stand on this "Platform"?

Before 1872, candidates for Parliament in England were nominated on a platform known as the "hustings," from which they made their speeches to the voters. Today, "to be out on the hustings" means to be out actively campaigning for election. A political party's policy proposals in an election campaign are called its "platform." Each specific proposal or part of the "platform" is called a "plank."

Sacrificial Lambs

A constituency that always elects a candidate for the same political party is called a "safe seat." Candidates for other parties who run in these safe seats are sometimes called "sacrificial lambs." They run so their party will be represented, but they know they cannot win. They are sacrificed to the political system and agree to do it like lambs.

WHAT DOES A
POLITICAL
PARTY LOOK
LIKE?

Each political party has a constitution — a set of rules that it follows to make decisions and solve problems. Political parties also have a structure. Usually this structure is called an executive, with different people elected by the members of the party for one or two years at a time to do specific jobs. In general, they work for free at these positions, although the presidents of the national political parties usually receive a salary.

The main responsibility of the executive is to work with the party membership from across the country on policy and election strategy. For instance, the Secretary looks after all of the correspondence (letter writing) and minutes (written record) of each meeting. The Treasurer is responsible for all of the financial and money matters in the party. The President works closely with the parliamentary caucus of MPs and Senators. This person also travels to as many constituencies as possible across Canada to speak to party workers at conventions, parties and social events.

Each political party also has a parliamentary wing (section). This parliamentary wing is made up of the leader of the party, elected at a leadership convention by the party's delegates chosen from each constituency across Canada, and Members of Parliament and Senators. This group is also called the *caucus*. They meet regularly — every Wednesday morning when Parliament is in session — to discuss concerns they have about their constituencies and regions, or about federal government legislation that affects them. This meeting gives the Prime Minister and the Cabinet a first-hand report on what is happening in all the constituencies across the country.

The Whips Are On!

Sound like a Western movie? Not really. This is the expression used to tell us that MPs for each party in the House of Commons must vote as their parliamentary caucus has decided on the legislation being considered. Sometimes an MP votes against a motion caucus has agreed to support. If it is a matter of great importance, then that MP may be disciplined. Certain privileges could be removed, either for a short time or permanently. After a problem has been discussed in Cabinet and a solution found, Cabinet Ministers must support that decision even if they disagree with it. (This is called "Cabinet solidarity.") Cabinet

Ministers who go against the government on any matter must resign their posts. The same applies to Parliamentary Secretaries and MPs who hold other important parliamentary positions.

Electoral Highlights

In 1867 – Men over the age of 21 who were British subjects, who owned land in their electoral district and who were on the voters' list were the only persons eligible to vote in a federal election.

In 1918 – Women could vote for the first time in a federal election.

In 1960 – Aboriginals living on reserves could vote for the first time.

In 1975 – British citizens living in Canada could no longer vote at federal elections.

In 1987 – Every Canadian citizen 18 years of age or over who is on the voters' list can vote in a federal election.

Getting Elected

As was discussed earlier in the book, Members of Parliament are elected at least once every five years to represent the interests of people in a geographical area, called a constituency. Once elected, they work in the House of Commons, on constituency problems and on parliamentary committees. Some MPs have extra responsibilities as Cabinet Ministers, Parliamentary Secretaries or committee chairpersons. But who can run for Parliament, and how do they get elected?

MAKING THE DECISION TO RUN FOR THE HOUSE OF COMMONS

Any Canadian citizen who is 18 years of age or over on election day can be a candidate in a federal (national) election. In 1988, I decided to run for Parliament. This was not an easy decision for me, as my spouse was already a senior Cabinet Minister and our daughter was only 11 years old. After much discussion, though, we all agreed that it was a good idea, and my family all pitched in to help with campaigning, babysitting and household duties.

WINNING YOUR PARTY'S NOMINATION

First, I had to be elected as a candidate for my party. To do this, I had to run against two other people, (who also wanted to be the P.C. candidate) at a *nominating convention*. Remember that each political party has their own nominating convention to choose someone in each of the federal constituencies (ridings) to be their *official candidate*. Before the meeting, my family and other supporters worked hard selling memberships to people who wanted me to be the candidate. They were then entitled to vote at the official nominating convention, which took place in Ottawa.

WHAT HAPPENS AT THE NOMINATING CONVENTION

At the nominating convention, all three of the candidates gave a speech outlining why they wanted to be the party's official candidate, and why they would be the best choice. Then the *delegates* to the convention, who were those who had bought a membership card, voted. I was elected on the first ballot, with a clear majority. If I had not been, or if there had been more people running, then the person

with the least number of votes would have been required to drop off the list, and the people would have voted again. When a clear majority (50 percent + 1) was declared for one candidate, then that person would become the party's official candidate, and their name would be submitted to the party leader for formal approval. They can then get money and helpers from party headquarters, and special tax provisions will apply for raising campaign funds.

ORGANIZING FOR THE ELECTION

The day after the nominating convention, I put together an *election campaign team* to help me run an effective election campaign. Many people are needed to run an election campaign in each riding. Among the key people I chose were:

☞ a *campaign manager* to run the campaign;
☞ a *finance and fundraising director* to raise the money we needed for the campaign;

☞ an *official agent* to watch over the accounting for all our expenses;

☞ a *legal counsel* to explain the *Elections Act* to us;

☞ a *head of volunteers* and a *youth director* to take charge of all the people who wanted to work in many different ways on the campaign;

☞ a *scheduling director* to prepare my daily campaign activities;

☞ an *office manager* to run the campaign headquarters. We set up campaign headquarters in two places, as the riding was large, and had both rural and urban parts.

THE WRIT PERIOD

During the election period (also called the *writ period*), I worked very hard to meet as many of my constituents (voters) as possible. I did this by:

- ☞ knocking on doors;
- ☞ being on television, radio and in the newspapers;
- ☞ going to local events, like fairs, bazaars and seniors' homes;
- ☞ sending out mailings to people, explaining my stand on issues;
- ☞ attending all-candidates meetings;
- ☞ making speeches to many groups, such as the Rotary Club, women's organizations, Chambers of Commerce and others;
- ☞ campaigning wherever there were voters — at bus stops, in shopping centres, at bingo games and in people's living rooms;
- ☞ putting signs on lawns throughout the riding, and in prominent places, to show support.

ELECTION DAY

Election day is full of excitement. Usually, the candidate votes early in the morning and spends the day visiting the many *polling places* (also called *polling stations*) in the riding, to greet people and thank volunteers working on her/his campaign. The candidate can also vote at an *advance poll* (as I did). Like it sounds, an advance poll is one which is set up ahead of the election day to allow people who know they will be away on election day to vote.

At each polling station, each official political party can have a *scrutineer*. Scrutineers ensure that all the rules are followed, and that the election is fair. They also stay and watch as the votes are counted.

Each eligible voter comes to their assigned polling station — usually in their neighbourhood — and is given a ballot. They then vote by putting an "X" beside the name of the candidate of their choice.

If there are problems, the scrutineers tell the *Electoral Officer* responsible for their riding. This is a person who has special training in how elections are to be properly conducted. In extreme situations, the decision of the Electoral Officer can be appealed (challenged) by going to court.

AFTER THE VOTE

The person with the most votes (not necessarily a majority) becomes the *elected Member of Parliament* for that riding, and will represent the people (constituents) in that riding for the next five years. She/he is referred to as the "elected representative of the people."

I did not win my own election campaign, and while I was very disappointed, it was still an excellent experience.

It allowed me the opportunity to be actively involved in parliamentary democracy at the electoral level, and to encourage many others — especially women and youth — to work on an election campaign. Many did so for the first time, and as a result of this experience, we now have many more people who understand how to run an election campaign, and may, someday, even be candidates themselves.

Something To Do

Everything about Elections

Did you ever wonder how people know where and when to vote? Would you like to see what a ballot looks like? Why not hold your own mock (pretend) election at home or at school with your friends? Maybe, when you are having elections for class president or school executive, you could use the rules set out in the *Elections Act*, and see for yourself how a real election works.

The Chief Electoral Officer in Ottawa has a complete kit available for free that will tell you all you need to know about federal election campaigns. And if you still have questions, perhaps you could invite your MP to come to your school to give you the answers.

For a copy of the following booklets or pamphlets, write to: Elections Canada, Ottawa, Canada, K1A OM6.

☞ Representation in the Federal Parliament
☞ Canada's Electoral System
☞ Voter's Guide
☞ Student Voter's Guide
☞ Voting in Canada
☞ Your Returning Officer
☞ My Favourite Playmate (grades K-3)
☞ Canada at the Polls (election simulation kit).

Pork Barrelling

Another word for political patronage is "pork barrelling." Both of these terms are used to describe large-scale political favours offered by a government in return for money, votes or other resources. Modern communications have made this practice better known and harder to hide, but the practice has always existed.

Who Can Vote?

Every Canadian citizen who is at least 18 years of age by voting day and is on the voters' list can vote at federal elections. Prisoners, the mentally incompetent and people who might be asked to vote to break a tie between two candidates cannot vote. The tie-breakers include the Chief Electoral Officer, his/her deputies in each constituency (called local returning officers) and federal judges. Because of the Charter of Rights, judges and prisoners may soon be allowed to vote.

What Is a Poll?

When used in the electoral sense, a poll means the place where people vote. It is also called a polling station. On election day, people "go to the polls," which means they are voting. Do you know other meanings this word can have?

The Charter of Rights and Freedoms

EVERY REAL DEMOCRACY has certain fundamental (basic) rights and freedoms that are guaranteed to its citizens. It is the legal guarantee of these rights and freedoms that sets our system of government apart from other political systems in the world. Since 1982, our fundamental rights and freedoms have been set out in the *Charter of Rights and Freedoms* (often simply called "the Charter").

WHAT IS A
FUNDAMENTAL
RIGHT?

A fundamental right is an essential part of each of us. Without it, we are less free and able to live the kind of life we should be able to live in a democracy. Each day, we enjoy our fundamental rights without even thinking about them. For instance, think about the freedom to speak and the freedom of movement. How often do we stop and worry about what we say? Have you ever criticized what persons in authority — such as the government or the police — were doing? If so, did you realize how lucky you were to live in a democratic country where you need not worry about being arrested and put in jail for your remarks?

Do you sometimes go on holidays outside of Canada? If you do, have you ever had to wait for permission from the Canadian government before you could leave? If you are a Canadian citizen, you have a fundamental right of free movement. No one tells you where you can go in Canada or stops you from travelling to other countries.

We are so used to living in a free country that we often take these rights and freedoms for granted. We forget that many people in the world do not have all of these privileges. And by forgetting our good fortune of being Canadians, living in a big, beautiful and free country, we sometimes pretend that these rights and freedoms will always be ours, no matter what happens. But, of course, that is not so.

We should think of our democratic rights and freedoms as being like a rare and precious flower. We are the gardeners who are responsible for its safety and continued growth. If we take care of our flower, it will not fade or be trampled by others or broken by a vicious storm. If it is our privilege to have this beautiful flower in our garden, it is also our responsibility to take good care of it.

THE CANADIAN BILL OF RIGHTS, 1960

Our fundamental rights and freedoms were not always guaranteed by law. When he was elected Prime Minister in 1957, John Diefenbaker had one very important goal. As a young boy growing up in Saskatchewan, he had belonged to neither of Canada's official language groups. The Diefenbaker family did not come from France or Great Britain, but from Germany. Because he had felt discrimination as a young man, he resolved that when he became Prime Minister, he would introduce a Canadian bill of rights. This he did, in 1960. Mr. Diefenbaker's *Canadian Bill of Rights* served as our guide to our democratic rights and freedoms until Parliament passed

The Constitution Act, 1982, with its entrenched *Charter of Rights and Freedoms.*

THE CHARTER OF
RIGHTS AND
FREEDOMS

In 1981, then-Prime Minister Pierre Trudeau introduced in Parliament a constitutional bill which would allow Canadians to amend our own Constitution in Canada. Until then, our Constitution could only be amended with the consent of the Parliament of Great Britain. As part of that bill, the government proposed a *Charter of Rights and Freedoms* that would be *entrenched* in (embedded in and made a part of) our Constitution. This was an important improvement over the 1960 Bill of Rights. It meant that certain fundamental rights guaranteed in the Charter could only be changed by Parliament and a majority of the Legislatures using a specific "amending formula." The Bill of Rights, by contrast, could be amended by an Act of Parliament, passed with a simple majority.

Because this was such an important constitutional proposal, Parliament spent months debating it in the House of Commons and in Committee. They argued about what was the best possible wording for the Act itself and for the Charter. Many changes were made to improve and change the original bill.

All of the provinces except Quebec signed the 1981 Constitutional Accord. Since then, the federal government has been trying to reach a solution to Quebec's concerns that would allow its government to join the federal and other governments in Canada's constitutional family. Canada's Constitution is a "living" document, which is always growing and changing, just as Canada grows and changes. The federal and provincial governments are always working to ensure that the Constitution — which embodies our values and democratic principles — remains a current and effective document. The courts assist in this work by interpreting legislation and ensuring that all the laws passed by Parliament and the Legislatures respect the rights and freedoms guaranteed in our Constitution.

Something To Do

Find Out about Your Rights

If you would like more information about your rights, you can do one of the following things.

☞ Contact your Member of Parliament and ask for a copy of the government booklet entitled: *The Charter of Rights and Freedoms: A Guide for Canadians.*

☞ Write to the Canadian Human Rights Commission. In Ottawa their address is: Canadian Human Rights Commission • 257 Slater Street • Ottawa, Ontario • K1A 1E1. They can tell you about the regional office nearest you.

☞ If you need information on the rights of women, contact: The Canadian Advisory Council on the Status of Women • 18th Floor • 66 Slater Street • P.O. Box 1541, Station B • Ottawa, Ontario • K1P 5R5.

☞ If your question is about language rights, write to the Commissioner of Official Languages at: 66 Slater Street • Ottawa, Ontario • K1A 0T8. They will be able to give you more information about their regional offices.

WHO IS
PROTECTED
BY THE CHARTER?

The Charter only covers relationships between an individual and governments. This would include government bodies like the police (RCMP), the Courts or Crown corporations (for example, Air Canada or CN). Provincial human rights legislation still deals with issues of discrimination between individuals, where the government is not directly involved. For instance, if you are denied an apartment because of your colour, sex or ethnic origin, you would call the provincial Human Rights Commission and proceed under the provincial legislation.

WHAT
FUNDAMENTAL
RIGHTS AND
FREEDOMS ARE
PROTECTED?

The following is a brief look at the rights and freedoms guaranteed in the Charter. Section 2 of the *Constitution Act, 1982,* sets out the fundamental freedoms that are guaranteed to every Canadian under the Charter. These are:

1. *Freedom of conscience and religion.* This means that we are free to worship in the religion of our choice. It also means that we are free not to worship at all, if we choose.

2. *Freedom of thought, belief, opinion and expression,* including freedom of the press and other communications media. This means that unless the media report something that is untrue no person or government can prevent them from reporting on everything that happens in Canada.

3. *Freedom of peaceful assemblies.* This means that we can meet anywhere as a group, in public or in private, as long as we do so peacefully and without violence.

4. *Freedom of association.* This means that we can be with whichever friends we choose — the government cannot tell us whom we may or may not see.

Section 3 of the Charter sets out every qualified Canadian's right to vote.

Section 4 requires that all democratically elected governments (both federal and provincial) must hold a general election at least once every five years. The exception is in the case of "real or apprehended war, invasion or insurrection." In such emergencies, the House of Commons or a Legislature may be continued beyond the five-year limit, but only if this continuation is not opposed by more than one-third of the MPs or Members of the Legislative Assembly.

Section 5 of the Charter requires that all governments meet and pass laws at least once during every 12-month period.

WHAT OTHER
RIGHTS ARE
PROTECTED?

There are also other rights and freedoms protected by the Charter. These include:

☞ Mobility rights. All Canadian citizens have the right to live and work in any province of Canada. They also have the right to enter, remain in or leave Canada whenever they choose.

☞ Legal rights. These are guarantees that protect the basic right of all living Canadians to "life, liberty and security." For instance, Canadians cannot be arrested or imprisoned on another person's whim.

There must be a reason for the arrest, and they must be told what that reason is. Further, if Canadians are arrested or detained by the police, they must be told of their right to see a lawyer and can refuse to give information — called evidence — until they have actually spoken with their lawyer. Canadians cannot be held without being told what specific offence they are charged with, and must be tried (go before a judge and/or jury) within a reasonable time of being charged or arrested. Finally, in our system of democracy, Canadians must be assumed innocent until proven guilty of an offence by a judge and/or jury, and cannot be charged and tried twice for the same offence. Before and during a trial, Canadians

can have an interpreter if they are deaf or do not understand the language of the proceedings.

☞ Equality rights. Section 15 (1) makes it an offence to discriminate against any Canadian on the basis of race, national or ethnic origin, colour, religion, sex, age or because he or she has a mental or physical disability. This section became law on April 17, 1985.

Section 15 (2) specifically provides for Affirmative Action programs. This means that governments, companies or educational institutions can start special programs to ensure that groups who have been excluded in the past have the chance to participate more fully in Canadian society. Among such groups are Aboriginal peoples, the disabled, women and new Canadians.

Something To Do

A Charter Fit for Framing

For your own free copy of Canada's *Charter of Rights and Freedoms*, suitable for framing, write to:

Secretary of State
The Communications Directorate
10th Floor, 25 Eddy Street
Hull, Quebec
K1A 0M5

Turning Over a New LEAF

Women knew that having a Constitution that guaranteed their rights was not enough. They also had to ensure that the courts interpreted the legislation as Parliament intended it. It is very expensive to take a case through the court system. For instance, it could cost as much as a quarter of a million dollars to take a case all the way to the Supreme Court of Canada.

To ensure that women had a chance to be heard, a group of people from across Canada — many of them women lawyers — founded a group called the Legal Education and Action Fund (LEAF). Its mandate is to take to court Charter cases involving sexual discrimination against women.

For more information on LEAF, write to:
Legal Education and Action Fund (LEAF)
344 Bloor Street West, Suite 403
Toronto, Ontario
M5S 1W9

BILINGUALISM AND MULTI-CULTURALISM

In Canada, the official languages are English and French. Section 23 makes certain guarantees about minority language educational rights. This section is important to all of us. It sets out the main rules that determine your right, if you are in an English or French-speaking minority in your province, to be taught in your own language.

Canada is often described as a bilingual country in a multicultural setting. Except for the Aboriginal peoples, all Canadians are immigrants. All of our families came here from somewhere else. My own family came to Canada in the middle of the nineteenth century to escape from famine in Ireland.

Today, new Canadians come from every corner of the world. Some come to be with family members who have already settled here. Some come as political refugees, fleeing a bad government in their own country. Some come to find work or to study. Others just come because they have heard that Canada is a great country in which to live and grow.

The multicultural nature of Canada presents governments and individual Canadians with an enormous challenge. We have, in the Charter (and in provincial and federal human rights legislation), laws that protect people from discrimination based on colour, race and country of origin. But the real test for us will be to see if we are mature, kind and thoughtful enough as a people to live together and build a truly great country. We must build upon the many strengths of our varied backgrounds and cultures. If we can do this, it will make Canada much stronger than any Charter or human rights legislation ever could.

THE 1987 CONSTITUTIONAL ACCORD

This Accord is better known as *The Meech Lake Accord*. It was signed on June 3, 1987, by the Prime Minister and the ten provincial Premiers. It was named for the beautiful lake in the Gatineaus where their negotiations took place. This Accord had a special purpose — to finish the work begun by the *repatriation process* in 1982. One of the most important tasks was to make it possible for Quebec to become a full member of Canada's constitutional family. To do that, the Accord proposed several changes to the Constitution, including:

- ☞ The recognition of Canada's linguistic duality as a historical reality;
- ☞ The recognition that Quebec constitutes within Canada a distinct society;
- ☞ The maintenance of the existing powers, rights and privileges of Parliament and all the Legislatures, including those relating to language;
- ☞ The interpretations to be given to these recognitions would not affect those already within the Constitution concerning the multicultural heritage of Canadians or of Aboriginal peoples.
- ☞ That Senators be chosen from among a list provided by the provinces. This allowed Alberta to conduct an election for a Senate seat available in that province.
- ☞ That responsibility for immigration be shared between the federal government and the provinces. Where there was a disagreement, the federal laws would prevail (be followed).
- ☞ That the Supreme Court be an institution enshrined in our Constitution. At least three of the nine Justices would be appointed from Quebec, and be trained in the civil law. In Canada, the English provinces would follow the British Common Law system, as a former British colony, while Quebec has a Civil Code — like most of the countries of Europe and Latin America.

☞ That provinces be able to choose not to join new national shared-cost programs, imposed in areas where the provinces have exclusive provincial authority (i.i. under s. 92 of the *Constitution Act*). However, if they had their own program, they had to follow the national objectives if they were to receive money from the federal government to run them. This was referred to as *opting out*.

☞ That the Prime Minister hold a meeting, once a year, with all the provincial Premiers. This would confirm the practice of *First Ministers' Conferences*, which are already held in Canada annually to discuss important questions.

☞ That the amending formula be changed to require *unanimity* (i.e. Parliament and all the provinces had to agree) in all cases requiring major changes in Canada's institutions, such as the Senate, Parliament, the Supreme Court, or for the creation of new provinces.

☞ That the Prime Minister be required to hold a special First Ministers' Constitutional Conference at least once a year, beginning in 1988, on Senate reform, the fisheries and other matters of importance to Canadians.

THE
FAILURE OF
MEECH LAKE

While the Accord was adopted after much discussion amongst the Prime Minister and the provincial Premiers, and with the help of hundreds of public servants, after massive lobbying from interest groups across Canada, it still had another bridge to cross before becoming part of our Constitution. The federal and provincial leaders agreed to seek the adoption of this constitutional amendment by Parliament and all the provincial legislative assemblies within three years.

Once they had all adopted an identical constitutional amendment, it would become part of Canada's Constitution, and be called *The Constitutional Amendment, 1987*. The process began with its acceptance by the Legislature of Quebec.

But as Canadians know, the *Meech Lake Accord* resulted in bitter debates and divisions. Not all the provinces carried through on their commitment within the required three-year period, and, consequently, the Accord did not become part of Canada's Constitution.

THE 1992
CHARLOTTETOWN
AGREEMENT

The failure of the Meech Lake Accord did not end the need for Constitutional discussions and reforms. Several questions needed to be resolved, including Quebec's participation as a full constitutional partner in the Canadian federation. The public debate about the Meech Lake Accord had also shown that many other groups and interests wanted their concerns voiced at the same time. This required a discussion which would be later referred to as the *Canada Round* of constitutional negotiations because they included so many other questions beyond that of Quebec's participation and role in Canada.

The constitutional amendment which resulted from this process was called the *Charlottetown Accord*, as the final document was signed by all the leaders of the participating governments and groups on August 28, in Charlottetown, P.E.I., a place referred to as the cradle of Confederation. Indeed, all the leaders at that meeting were conscious of the historic nature of both the place where they had gathered and the document they had drafted.

For the first time in Canada's history, this constitutional conference included not only leaders from the federal and provincial governments, but also from the Yukon, the Northwest Territories, the Assembly of First Nations, the Inuit Tapirisat of Canada, the Native Council of Canada and the Métis National Council. When they signed the Accord in late August 1992, they did so unanimously. Never before in Canada's history had this happened.

WHAT THE
AGREEMENT
PROPOSED

The 1992 Charlottetown Agreement was the product of the Canada Round of constitutional negotiations. As such, it was lengthy and complex, covering many issues. Under five general headings, it proposed many fundamental changes to make Canada's Constitution and institutions, such as Parliament, the courts and the justice system, better able to meet the new realities and needs of Canadians living in the modern world.

1. The Canada Clause

☞ A *Canada Clause*, which set out fundamental Canadian values, including our commitment to parliamentary democracy, linguistic duality, individual and human rights, equality between women and men, respect for Canada's Aboriginal peoples, the recognition of Quebec as a distinct society within Canada, racial and ethnic equality, and the protection of official language minority groups across Canada. This clause would also help the courts, as they interpret laws, to ensure that they respect the principles and provisions of the *Charter of Rights and Freedoms.*

2. Parliamentary Reform

☞ An elected Senate, made up of an equal number from each province, and one from each of the Yukon and the Northwest Territories, with some provinces committing themselves to gender equality as well.

☞ The setting of the number of provincial seats in the House of Commons to better reflect the population. This would offset the imbalance created by having a Senate where each province had the same number of Senators, regardless of their population. As before, the provision protecting provinces with a smaller population was maintained; no province could have fewer seats than another province with a smaller population. For example, P.E.I., with under 150,000 people, has 4 seats; New Brunswick and Nova Scotia each have ten. The Agreement also guaranteed a minimum of 25 percent of the House of Commons seats for Quebec, (it now has more than that), in part to replace the 18 seats they (and Ontario) would lose in order to make the elected Senate "equal," with the same number from each province, regardless of their population.

☞ The entrenchment of the Supreme Court as an institution in our Constitution, with three of the nine judges from the Quebec civilist tradition.

3. A Social and Economic Union

☞ The description of a set of social "policy objectives," (not enforceable by the courts), on environmental protection, universal health care, social programs and benefits, education, and workers' rights.

☞ A separate political accord to address the question of an economic union (or Canadian "common market") to allow for the free trade of goods and services across the provinces in Canada.

4. The Division of Powers

☞ All provinces would have equal powers.

☞ The federal spending powers would be limited, so that provinces "opting out" of national shared-cost programs in areas of exclusively provincial jurisdiction (such as education or health) would be able to have their own programs funded, but only if they conformed to the national standards and objectives.

☞ Certain powers, such as immigration and labour force training, for instance, would pass to the provinces, if they wanted that power.

☞ The decentralization of some of the powers to the provinces, including those concerning culture (although Ottawa is still responsible for national cultural agencies).

☞ The federal government would not involve itself (also called "vacating the field") in the provincial jurisdictions of mining, forestry, recreation and tourism, housing and municipal and urban affairs.

5. Aboriginal Self-Government

☞ The principle of an inherent right to aboriginal self-government, within Canada, was accepted by all the leaders. It was a sign of respect for Aboriginal peoples, and an attempt to give them control over their own lives and communities. No one definition of self-government was ever agreed to, and a five-year limit was set to allow for extensive discussions on how it would be achieved.

☞ The federal and provincial governments committed themselves to negotiating the details of Aboriginal self-government.

THE REFERENDUM AND REJECTION OF THE CHARLOTTETOWN AGREEMENT

After the Charlottetown Agreement was signed unanimously by the 17 federal, provincial, Territorial and Aboriginal leaders on August 28, the Quebec government changed its original plan for a referendum on sovereignty to one on the Agreement. British Columbia and Alberta also decided to hold provincial referendums. The federal government then decided to hold one national referendum, on October 26, 1992. The question asked of Canadians was:

"Do you agree that the Constitution of Canada should be renewed on the basis of the agreement reached on August 28, 1992?"

After a bitter, divisive and difficult two months, the majority of Canadians voted "No." Today, the issues addressed by both these constitutional amendments remain unresolved; a separatist government has been elected in the province of Quebec; and Quebecers will be asked in 1995 whether or not they want to leave Canada and form a new country.

This is a very troubling and important time in Canada's history. It is also very important to our lives, too. We should all spend some time thinking about how we can contribute to Canada's future unity and stability. It is not enough for us to be against certain ideas and proposals. We must also be ready to propose other ways to keep Canada strong and free.

❦

As Canadian citizens, we all have a responsibility to do what we can to better understand each other's concerns, and to work to keep Canada strong and united. Think about some of the things that you or your class might do to encourage more links and communication among other young people in other parts of Canada.

Contact your local paper and television. Publicize your efforts. Use the tools of modern technology. How about becoming "video pen pals" with students living somewhere else in Canada? Or how about sending special greetings by cassette? There are many things we can all do to increase our understanding of each other as Canadians. List some of your own suggestions, and see how you can do your part to make other Canadians part of your own family and community.

❦

A Glossary of Parliamentary Terms

act

A law or a statute.

adjournment

The end of the sitting of the House of Commons or Senate until the next day or some later day — for example, until after the Christmas break or the summer recess. (How is this different from *prorogation* and *dissolution*? Check these words and see.)

amendment

A change proposed or made to a motion or a bill. It can be a proposal to add, leave out or change some words. An amendment can even give the original motion or bill a completely new sense or meaning.

backbencher

See *private Member.*

ballot

A piece of paper used for voting. On election day you put an "X" on the ballot beside the name of the candidate of your choice.

bill

The draft of a law, presented in either the House of Commons or the Senate. Also called an act. The bill will become law if it passes the House of Commons and the Senate and receives Royal Assent.

budget

The document that contains the government's financial plans, usually for the coming one-year period.

bureaucracy

All the people who work in the departments of government, carrying out Parliament's programs and policies. Also called the *Public Service.*

by-elections

Extra elections held in particular constituencies between two general elections. A vacancy (freeing up of a constituency) can occur because a Member of Parliament has died, retired or been expelled.

Cabinet	The body of Ministers chosen by the Prime Minister, usually from among elected Members of Parliament of his or her own party. In rare circumstances, Senators and private citizens can also be named to Cabinet.
caucus	All the Members of Parliament and Senators from a political party. Also refers to the meetings the three national parties have every Wednesday morning in Ottawa when Parliament is sitting.
Chief Electoral Officer (Canada)	The public servant who is responsible for the fair conduct of all federal general elections and by-elections under the *Canada Elections Act.*
Clerk of the House of Commons/Clerk of the Senate	The chief permanent officers of both Houses, who are experts on parliamentary procedure. They advise Speakers, Members of Parliament and Senators when asked to do so.
closure	The procedure by which debate may be ended by a majority vote in the House, even when all Members wishing to speak have not done so.
constituency	An area that has its own Member of Parliament in the House of Commons. Also called a *riding.*
constitution	In its widest sense, the whole legal system of government of a country. In Canada, we speak of our Constitution as the *Constitution Act, 1982*, which includes the *Charter of Rights and Freedoms*. There are also many parliamentary traditions and customs which are unwritten, but which form part of how we are governed.
"crossing the floor"	This occurs when a Member of Parliament changes his or her political party and "crosses the floor" of the House of Commons to sit as a member of another party or as an Independent.

debate	The speeches and comments made by Members of Parliament or Senators from all political parties on the strengths and weaknesses of a bill, motion or other question that is presented to Parliament for its consideration.
division	In both the House of Commons and the Senate, all questions are decided by a vote. A simple majority is required to carry a question. There are two kinds of votes. One is a *voice* vote, where Members shout yes or no (aye or nay) to the question; the other is a *recorded* vote. This recorded vote is called a division, and the name of each Member of Parliament who voted for and against the question is recorded by the Clerk.
dissolution	The ending of a Parliament either because the Prime Minister has decided to call an election or because the government has been defeated on an important vote of confidence in the House of Commons. Normally an election is then held to elect a new House of Commons. (See also *adjournment* and *prorogation*.)
election	The actual procedure when eligible Canadians vote (go to the polls) to elect one representative from each federal constituency. An election must be held at least once every five years.
federal system	The division of power and special relationship between the national (federal) government, the ten provincial governments and the two territorial governments. Each level has certain rights and responsibilities.
Governor General	The Queen's representative in Canada and our Head of State. The Governor General prorogues and dissolves Parliament and must assent to all bills before they can

become law. At the provincial level, the Queen's representatives are called Lieutenant Governors.

Hansard The daily verbatim (word-for-word) record of the debates and speeches given in the House of Commons by Members of Parliament and in the Senate by Senators. The rough draft is called the "Blues" (not to be confused with the hockey team!) because it is typed on blue paper. While the "Blues" may be corrected, a Member of Parliament cannot change the meaning or actual wording of what was said.

Head of State In Canada, the Governor General is our Head of State.

House Leaders The three Members of Parliament chosen by their respective party leaders to set the Commons timetable for the introduction and passage of bills.

House of Commons The elected House of Parliament, sometimes called the Lower House. People elected to the House of Commons are called *Members of Parliament (MPs)*. (See also *Parliament*.)

Leader of the Opposition The person who leads the party with the second largest number of Members of Parliament in the House of Commons. Also called the Leader of Her Majesty's Loyal Opposition. The Leader of the Opposition in the Senate is appointed by the Leader of the Opposition in the Commons.

Legislature The body of elected provincial representatives who are responsible for passing laws at the provincial level. Also the name given to the building where they meet. Provincial representatives are called *Members of the Legislative Assembly* (MLA), *Members of the National*

113

Assembly (MNA), *Members of the Provincial Parliament* (MPP), or *Members of the House of Assembly* (MHA), depending on the province. Do you know what the tradition is in your province?

lobbying

Presenting your point of view to Members of Parliament or Senators for the purpose of influencing their vote or decision.

Member of Parliament (MP)

The person elected in each federal constituency to represent his or her constituents in the House of Commons.

Parliament

The national law-making body of Canada, made up of the Queen (represented by the Governor General), an elected House of Commons and an appointed Senate.

Prime Minister (PM)

The person who leads the party with the largest number of elected Members in the House of Commons. The head of government.

private Member

Any Member of Parliament who is not a Cabinet Minister, a Parliamentary Secretary or a committee chairperson is usually referred to as a private Member. Also called a *backbencher*.

Privy Council

The formal advisory body to the Crown (Queen). Membership is for life and includes former and present federal Cabinet Ministers, Governors General, some provincial premiers and former Speakers of the House and Senate.

prorogation

The term used to describe the end of a session of Parliament. When Parliament prorogues, all parliamentary business comes to an end. Bills remaining on the order paper "die" and must be re-introduced in the next session of Parliament. (See also *adjournment, dissolution.*)

Public Service	See *bureaucracy*.
Question Period	The time set aside in the House of Commons each day for questions to be put to government Ministers by other Members of Parliament. The same event happens in the Senate.
quorum	The exact number of members of a legislative body (such as Parliament) who must be present before that body is allowed to conduct business (such as passing laws).
readings	The stages of legislative approval required for the passage of all bills.
redistribution	Changing the boundaries of constituencies to take into account population growth and changes. This is usually done nationally about every ten years after the Census, when every person resident in Canada is officially counted.
Responsible Government	A system in which the Cabinet is responsible to Parliament, and through Parliament to the people. The Cabinet must always keep the confidence of a majority of the House of Commons or resign and be replaced.
riding	The popular word for *constituency*.
Royal Assent	The approval by the Governor General of legislation passed by Parliament. Unless a bill states otherwise, the date on which Royal Assent is given is the date on which the bill becomes law.
Senate	The appointed or Upper House of the Parliament of Canada.
shadow cabinet	The official opposition party spokespersons, each of whom is responsible for asking questions of one particular Cabinet Minister.

Speaker	The presiding officer who chairs the sessions of Parliament and makes sure its parliamentary rules are followed by all the Members.
Speech from the Throne	The document that sets out the general policy and legislative plans of the government for a new session of Parliament.
Standing Orders	The codified rules of procedure of the House of Commons. In the Senate, they are called the *Rules of the Senate*.
vote of non confidence	The government must always have the support of the majority of Members in the House of Commons in order to stay in power. If it is defeated on an important matter — such as a budget — then it must resign. This is called a vote of non confidence.
Whip	The Member of Parliament in each party who is responsible for making sure that there are always enough party members present for votes in Parliament and on committees. The Whip also assigns all office space to Members.

🍁

INDEX